EINSTEIN'S LAS.

Rod O'Connor was born on the 28th May 1949 on the family's 'wheat and sheep' farm in Victoria Australia, adjacent to the 1300 square miles kilometers of forest and national park known as The Little Desert. Rod loved the farm, and he loved the bush. In drought times, kangaroos and emus would leave the forest and graze the family's wheat crop. But his father never complained; he considered it was their land too.

After education at Dimboola Memorial High School, Rod studied at the Australian National University and Monash University, completing a doctorate in experimental cognitive psychology under Ken Forster, as well as training in zoology and health economics. Later Dr. Rod became a consultant in healthcare research and development, his clients including the World Bank, the World Health Organisation, the Asian Development Bank, the Australian Commonwealth Department of Health and Family Services, GSK, Roche, Servier, and various other Governments, NGOs, and private agencies.

In addition to consulting, Dr. Rod O'Connor has been an Associate Professor in Public Health at the University of New South Wales, and Senior Research Associate at the National Centre for Health Program Evaluation (the University of Melbourne and Monash University). In 2004 he published *Measuring Quality of Life in Health*, see www.rodoconnorassoc.com for more information. He now lives in Sydney, Australia, and may be contacted via rod@rodoconnorassoc.com

*A new type of thinking is essential
if mankind is to survive.*

—ALBERT EINSTEIN, 1946

Contents

How Can We Think Better?......................................1

Grasping The World As A Snake Bites It's Tail 5

We learn linkages and how they work...............6

Feelings help find solutions too..........................18

We sometimes make mistakes............................20

We have found a way to reason well................26

Summary: examine the science............................30

Knowing People By Seeing Ourselves...................33

Reading minds with how *we* feel.......................35

Working with groups and leaders......................41

Understand intentionally....................................46

Summary: understand by inquiry, not gut.........47

Finding Happiness Via Time Travel......................51

In search of good feelings...................................51

We want 'more'..55

Reimagining the situation..................................57

Happiness maps..65

Why we destroy so readily............................70

Summary: assess long-term, and no lies...........71

A Brave Rabbit Shows Us What Is Right 73

The value of values 74

We need world-protecting ethics 75

How to install a new value?....................76

Animals are people 80

A stopping function 84

Summary: protect our living world..............85

All The Truth And Half The World...............89

All the truth...................................91

A moratorium on half the world 93

A New Type Of Thinking 97

Appendices 103

Appendix 1. A checklist for decisions 105

Appendix 2. Ways to improve ourselves........107

Bibliography 111

Acknowledgments

The author is indebted to the many people who have read this book and offered support, over fifty at least. To all, I offer my sincere thanks - this book is dense, but initially it verged on unreadable. I will make specific reference to only two - Colin Schoknecht, for his reading of earlier drafts, and supporting me in the idea that you aim to get most of the main ideas right, and then you let the academics stew over the details; and Professor Jeff Richardson, for perusing several later drafts and raising crucial questions that I am grateful for and needed to answer. To all the others that I should have named, please forgive me!

How Can We Think Better?

Early on the morning of the 20th May 1834, near a pond close to the pension Sieur Faultrier in Paris, two men exchanged pistol rounds over a beautiful woman. One was Evariste Galois, a passionate republican and gifted mathematician. He had worked through the night writing a new mathematics known as Group Theory - it describes the symmetries of physics and helps us understand the structure of the universe. Evariste was shot in the stomach. He lay unattended on the grass for several hours, then died the next day. He was twenty years old.[1]

Galois had a genius for explaining. His late-night brilliance added to the store of problem-solving mathematics and science that has passed on to later generations. Yet his thoughts and feelings caused him to act wildly. His involvement in dangerous politics had taken him to jail, and a love affair produced a violent death. It seems a human can be very bright, but still make disastrous choices.

This contradiction characterizes our species. We are brilliant yet destructive, we might call it 'the Galois paradox.' We majestically develop remarkable technologies, engineers take us into space, and biologists eradicate diseases. But at the same time, we decide in a way that is self-defeating, even suicidal. We maintain nuclear weapons, choose despotic leaders, engage in war, and destroy other species. We are clever like the deities of old, the ancient Greek, Norse, and Indian gods: inquisitive, creative, and ready to harm. We are so smart we could extinguish most of life on earth, along with ourselves.

Einstein's message

Einstein was worried about our problematic nature. On the 23rd June 1946, more than a hundred years after the death of Galois, he was interviewed by the New York Times in an article titled "The real problem is in the hearts of men." Here he gave what he called his "message." He said the atomic bomb had altered the nature of the world, and "a new type of thinking is essential if mankind is to survive and move to higher levels."[2] In essence, Einstein feared we lacked the wisdom to avoid what may destroy us, a concern he maintained for the rest of his life. In 1955, only days before his death, he signed the Russell–Einstein Manifesto, calling for international disputes to be resolved peacefully.

Since Einstein, people have continued to act dangerously. We have failed to control our poor decisions, making mistakes on a grand scale. To the threat of nuclear war, we have added the perils of environmental destruction and global warming. A traditional hazard has reappeared too - a viral disease pandemic - but we will recover from this (pandemics like COVID 19 have occurred before); in contrast, our people-made dangers threaten to end humanity.

While we face threats that could end us, and have done so for over seventy years, we carry on as before. The behavioral sciences have not found answers - researchers have discovered more about how our brains work, but not how to make decisions for the future. We lack a functional understanding of humankind, practical information that will help us repair and refine our thinking.

This book has been written to help provide that knowledge. It does not aim to be correct in every way but seeks to identify essential elements - those that tell why we harm so readily, and how we can stop destroying our beautiful living planet.

To produce the book, I examined the scientific literature. I collected studies of awareness, creativity, reasoning, emotion, and decision making. But I soon realized that these fragmented studies did not provide a complete picture of how we think and decide – they were too separate from the real world. So I expanded my search, and sought real-life reports of crucial decisions, as occur when life is threatened or at the magical point of a momentous discovery. I also recorded observations made by novelists and playwrights, and, where necessary, drew upon my own experiences.

Having assembled the material, I looked for order. I sought patterns showing how we form options and choose among them. I looked for clusters of elements working together, evidence of overarching decision processes.

And now, I made my first discovery. Whichever way I tried to understand the material, there was another formulation, and the same content, subtly changed in emphasis, could be made to fit that too. I found we have an extraordinary and seemingly unlimited capacity to gather 'relevant' information and 'make sense' of it. The historian E.H. Carr had noted something similar – he said facts are not like "fish on a fish-mongers slab" but like fish in a vast ocean, where what we catch depends on "where we fish and the tackle we use."[3] I would later recognize that this suppleness of mind is both our greatest strength and our most sublime weakness.

Four Russian dolls

Then I made another discovery. I realized the way we make sense changes with the material we are trying to understand. We reason one way if the information concerns the material world, another when trying to understand people, a third when managing the hopes and desires of our inner-self, and a fourth when our sense of right and wrong tells us what to do. These four thinking worlds lie nested within each other, like Russian dolls (*matryoshka*).

In the following, I report my findings. The material is dense: there is a lot to tell, and it is not always that easy to grasp. But our thought processes are extraordinary, the best inspired and magical, the worst terrifying. And in the weaving together of the various sources of knowledge and insight, there are truths about humans. I show how we can think better - and here lie the keys to save ourselves and nature too.

CHAPTER 1.

Grasping The World As A Snake Bites It's Tail

If we were born gods, we might know the location of every element of the universe and the rules that bind them; we would immediately understand the world and ourselves. But we are not. Each of us has to study what lies around us and make sense of it, so we can explain, predict, and decide what to do.

In this chapter, I will describe some of the fundamentals of how we come to know the material world, the world of 'things.' Then we will be aware of how smart we are, and the ways we have to become even brighter. And I will look at the down-side too - for though we have come far, we make errors, and we have to correct them.

We learn linkages and how they work

As soon as we are born, we start to make sense of our world. Babies look at events before being able to speak, and soon young children ask 'why?' We learn objects, events, causes, and consequences. David Hume said we "define a cause to be an object followed by another, and where all the objects, similar to the first, are followed by objects similar to the second."[4]

This all takes time. Helen Keller was deaf, blind, and unable to speak, and it was not until she was seven years old that her teacher placed Helen's hand under a stream of water and traced 'w-a-t-e-r' into the other. Later, Helen said she suddenly saw that the characters meant the wonderful cool something that was flowing over her hand, that words, objects, and sensations were all linked. She had realized what a written word was, and from now on, she knew.[5]

We don't only learn events and connections, we also learn how things make us feel - we experience emotions. We see a snake and our stomach is queasy, we feel anxious. Or we go to a party, our body feels light, and we are happy.

Feelings are physical as well as mental, aspects that seem different but are hard to separate. In the 19th Century, the psychologist William James observed, "if we fancy some strong emotion, and then try to abstract from our consciousness of it all the feelings of its bodily symptoms, we find we have nothing left behind."[6] Nowadays, we say that emotion is 'embodied.'

With experience, we learn the emotion of events and how they are connected, and we spontaneously use this knowledge to gain what we need - the fridge has run out of milk, so we walk to the corner shop and buy some.

We respond automatically in life-threatening situations too. When fire-fighters, the military, and critical care nurses are in familiar circumstances, they engage in what Gary Klein called "recognition-primed decision making." One course of action comes to mind, which they implement.[7]

Forming stories

We don't only acquire simple connections - two events following each other, such as flicking a switch brings light - we learn multiple links, ones that allow us to predict and plan. We learn the rules of chess, and the steps we must take to build a shed.

And once more, we use these accounts (which may be called steps, sequences, narratives, or stories) with a minimum of conscious thought. Chess Grandmaster Raul Capablanca won one hundred and sixty-eight games in a row, proceeding around a circle of players. When asked how he played so quickly and well, he said, "I see only one move ahead, but it is always the correct one."[8] Whether the matter is simple or elaborate, possible courses of action appear with little thinking, and we implement them.

Sometimes, though, we first test their feasibility. Gary Klein found that firemen would assess a plan by 'watching' it in their mind's eye. If the mental simulation showed no problems, they approved it; if there were problems, they made amendments until it worked.[9] I did the same when building a backyard shed - I imagined vertical poles placed in the ground and 'saw' the poles might rot, so I mentally changed to decay-resistant timber. When all was fine, I proceeded.

In most of daily life, we identify sequences of events and use them to guide our actions.

But what happens when dealing with problems that no-one has an answer to? For example, how do we find solutions to problems in mathematics and science?

Finding answers to difficult questions

In such cases, we usually prepare. The investigator learns what others have discovered (often through a review of the literature), and clarifies the research question (what is to be found). The matter may also be discussed with colleagues or students, to "have the problem more clearly and cleanly in one's head," as one mathematician put it.[10]

But after that, answers may again appear spontaneously. The great French polymath Henri Poincaré gave an example. He had been trying, with little success, to solve an issue with "fuschian functions," and decided to have a time-out and go caving. He later described what happened:

> I left Caen, where I was living, to go on a geological excursion [and] forgot my mathematical work. Having reached Coutances, we entered an omnibus. The moment I put my foot on the step the idea came to me, without anything in my former thoughts seeming to have paved the way for it, that the transformations I used to define the Fuschian functions were identical with those of non-Euclidean geometry. I did not verify the idea, I did not have the time, as upon taking my seat in the omnibus I went on with a conversation already commenced, but I felt a perfect certainty.[11]

The answer had appeared unexpectedly and fully formed; Poincaré later called it, "an illumination." And not only was the appearance of a solution surprising, so was its time of arrival.

This is typical of new ideas - they emerge at all sorts of occasions. One investigator noted that they arise, "when you are taking a shower, when you are sleeping, or when driving, there is really no standard approach."[12] Nobel prize-winning physicist Richard Feynman was in a queue at the Cornell cafeteria when someone spun a plate in the air. Later he observed:

> *I had nothing to do, so I started to figure out the motion of the rotating plate. Then I thought about how the electron orbits start to move in relativity. And before I knew it, this whole business that I got the Nobel prize for came from that piddling around with the wobbling plate.*[13]

This anecdote illustrates what can be the third feature of problem-solving discoveries - Feynman had used his imagination.

Imagination may be essential for solving a problem. Einstein thought so. He said, "imagination is more important than knowledge... imagination encircles the world" (he also stated it was his imagination, not data, that led to the Special Theory of Relativity).[14] And Feynman agreed. In discussing the problem of superconductivity, he said, "we don't need any more experiments... we need more imagination."[15]

Imagination is used elsewhere too, not just in physics. Theseus, in Shakespeare's *A Midsummer Night's Dream*, said, "Lovers and madmen have such seething brains, such shaping fantasies ... [these] apprehend more than cool reason ever comprehends."

Thinking in pictures

So what is imagination? It often refers to the exploration of a range of new and unusual ideas or different ways of proceeding, some of which may be quite far-fetched.

Imagination can involve thinking in pictures; indeed, the word "imagine" comes from the Latin *imaginare* "to picture to oneself." In fact, visualization is common. Mental images appear in our thoughts, memories, dreams, and when reading stories. They take up about a quarter of our mental activity,[16] about the same as thinking with words. We also use them to understand how mechanisms work (we rate our understanding of a device according to the ease with which we can visualize its components).[17]

Images often appear as a metaphor, and these can help us discover. The chemist August Kekule was dozing and saw a snake with its tail in its mouth - and realized the benzene molecule was circular.[18] The clue for the mechanical sewing machine also came from a mental image - the inventor Elias Howe had a dream about cannibals, and noticed they had holes through the points of their spears (which inspired him to place 'eyes' at the tips of sewing machines needles).[19] And Alfred Wegener developed his theory of continental drift by mentally watching continents move like icebergs.[20]

Visual metaphors have made discoveries in physics too. Einstein was about age sixteen, and trying to understand the implications of a finite speed to light, when he imagined riding on a light beam. Later, this became Special Relativity Theory. Einstein usually thought in pictures - he said his imagining consisted of "more or less clear images," while "words or the language, as they are written or spoken, do not seem to play any role in my [Einstein's] mechanisms of thought."[21]

Visual metaphors are also used to explain. The world of atoms was depicted as a solar system, until quantum theory made it obsolete. Then Richard Feynman came up with "Feynman diagrams,"[22] and the sub-atomic world was once again in pictures.

Nor are visual metaphors confined to science. Picasso's cubist ideas arose because a friend introduced him to Poincaré's book *Science and Hypothesis,* and a book by Esprit Jouffret about complex polyhedrals. These described how an object could be represented in four dimensions by projecting a succession of perspectives in two. Picasso was amazed by them, and they led to paintings such as 'Les Demoiselles d'Avignon' and 'Guernica.'[23]

Images appear to be fundamental to our thinking. They allow us to consciously investigate a course of action, or 'see' a possible mechanism. Our animal ancestors may have used metaphors to form plans and explanations; other animals may manipulate mental images too, and think in pictures as we do.

But metaphors are not only found in what we see; they also appear in other senses. Einstein said his thoughts were sometimes of a "muscular type,"[24] and Feynman expressed his insights to his students as sounds, in "whoops, glissandos, or patterns of drumbeats."[25]

Discovering with metaphors

Why are metaphors helpful? They seem to aid our understanding by offering the gist of a complex idea via one that is concrete and familiar. They suggest a mechanism based on one we already know.

I recall a popular science program on telomeres, regions of repetitive nucleotide sequences at the end of chromosomes that protect the chromosomes from deterioration. The narrator described them as similar to "the plastic bits on the end of shoelaces that stop them from fraying."[26]

Metaphors make it easy to form predictions, which we need to test a theory. For example, my Ph.D. research in the late 1960s concerned the nature of word recognition, and two models vied for attention: the 'search' model (going through a series of files), and the 'logogen' model (exciting a neuron until it fires). The two metaphors made different forecasts, and it was relatively simple to assess which was more supported. The metaphors meant I knew where to look.[27] Metaphors may also be hard to avoid. If the same natural laws apply everywhere, then the natural world may contain a limited set of mechanisms. Every object or event could be a metaphor for another.

But metaphors create problems too, for we may cling to them when they are no longer useful. The philosopher of science Thomas Kuhn proposed one set of ideas is dominant at a time, and this directs scientists in what to discover, for example, 'the world is like a clock.' Kuhn said this persists until finally, there is a 'paradigm shift' when the set of ideas changes, say to 'the world is like a computer.'[28] In other words, metaphors may be 'sticky.' Kuhn felt this did not impair scientific progress, but others disagreed. Karl Popper and Paul Feyerabend argued that new ideas are essential, that old ideas contaminate facts,[29] and scientists have to think outside prevailing notions.[30]

A second problem is that metaphors are by nature ambiguous - what is conveyed by the notion will depend on the audience. The German journalist Mappes-Niediek observed that "The EU means different things depending on your language and cultural background. To the British, it is a commonwealth, a free trade zone; to the Germans, a federal-state; to Austrians, an imperial monarchy; and to countries formerly part of Yugoslavia, a type of Yugoslavia."[31] We must take care that a metaphor is understood as intended.

But the most obvious limitation of metaphors became apparent when physicists tried to explain the behavior of tiny particles: no metaphor was found to be suitable. Researchers could not conceive how the sub-atomic world behaved; what they saw was at odds with everyday experience. Richard Feynman said about the quantum world, "do not keep saying to yourself, if you can possibly avoid it, 'but how can it be like that?' because you will go 'down the drain' into a blind alley from which nobody has yet escaped - nobody knows how it can be like that."[32]

In this situation, a different form of imagination was needed. Mathematics.

Has mathematics replaced metaphor?

Mathematics rescued science. It explained the sub-atomic world where other thinking did not; the equations were 'the one part people felt they could understand.'[33] And formulae *discovered* too. Paul Dirac used pure mathematics to formulate the Klein-Gordon field equations, which predicted the presence of an antimatter counterpart to the electron. Later, the "positron" was found.[34]

Mathematics has not only succeeded in the quantum world. The program BACON generated mathematical functions using the same data as Kepler, and found Kepler's Third Law (describing the motion of planets around the Sun).[35] And even when wrong, a mathematical idea may hint at possible discoveries. Gomo Shimura said approvingly of the young Japanese mathematician Yutaka Taniyama (1927–1958) that he made many mistakes, but they were 'very interesting' mistakes.[36]

Some say that only mathematics can express man's knowledge of nature (sometimes attributed to the German theoretical physicist Werner Heisenberg), but mathematical models are not always superior. In the 1920s, Heisenberg considered quantum physics purely in terms of mathematics while Erwin Schrodinger used wave imagery, and they arrived at similar answers.

Has mathematics superseded metaphors? Not for everyone. The biologist E.O. Wilson felt the best science didn't come from mathematical models and experiments, but from "a more primitive mode of thought, wherein the hunter's mind weaves ideas from old facts and fresh metaphors and the scrambled crazy images of things recently seen."[37] And Richard Feynman said that Einstein's ability to generate new ideas failed when he "stopped thinking in concrete visual images," and instead became, "a manipulator of equations."[38]

Metaphor and mathematics both have their place. The great James Clerk Maxwell thought so - he who unified light, magnetism, and electricity in formulating the mathematical basis of electromagnetic radiation, and with Newton and Einstein was one of the greatest physicists of all time. Maxwell said that science is equally valid, "whether it appears in the robust form and vivid coloring of a physical illustration, or in the tenuity and paleness of a symbolic representation."[39]

Overall, an answer can be revealed by a cause and effect sequence, a visual metaphor, or a mathematical expression. And whatever it's roots, the final form of an explanation is often a narrative, an account of connected events in order of happening. For as the paleontologist Stephen Jay Gould said, humans are "the primates who tell stories."[40]

Means for finding answers

We have investigated how answers appear. Are there tools that can help us generate ideas?

Probably the most fundamental aid to the right idea is experience, as it seems to develop intuition. French mathematician Jacques Hadamard said he was better than his students because of superior intuition (he said this helped him correct his errors).[41] Experience makes a difference in healthcare too; the diagnoses of medical experts are more accurate than novices because they make better initial hypotheses (while having similar textbook knowledge).[42] Presumably, greater experience means exposure to more explanatory mechanisms (connections and metaphors) and practice in applying them. Note that living in a foreign country also aids creativity,[43] as does having a partner from a different ethnic background.[44]

Assistance can come from spending time in bed. Gustav Fechner divined a law while about to sleep, 'Fechner's law' (the idea that subjective sensation is proportional to the logarithm of the stimulus intensity),[45] and August Kekule conceived the structure of benzene while dozing. Jacques Hadamard, too, reported "the sudden and immediate appearance of a solution at the very moment of sudden awakening."[46] I, also, have experienced new ideas in the muzzy state before dreaming - as problems float gently by, odd connections become plausible.

Why might drowsiness help new ideas emerge? Perhaps improbable explanations need disordered thought, which is safe when settled at night (but hazardous by day). It could also be because all of our processing capacity is now free to work on the problem.

But why not go all the way, and fall asleep? Dreams are a source of answers too.[47] Beethoven, Mozart, and Wagner all mentioned dreams as inspiring their compositions, and Robert Louis Stevenson said the plot for Dr. Jekyll and Mr. Hyde came in this way. Dreaming was also responsible for at least one mechanical invention - Elias Howe's sewing machine. On the other hand, sleeping doesn't seem to help with mathematical thinking. As reported by Jacques Hadamard, the mathematician Maillet surveyed sixty colleagues, and none said they had solved a mathematical problem with a dream.[48]

Another path to discovery is a way-out possibility - we can explore the link between our problem and *randomly chosen words*. A notorious Australian literary hoax suggests this way. In 1945, the literary journal *Angry Penguins* published a set of poems by supposed watch repairer "Ern Malley" (deceased). Critics were amazed by the virtuosity of the verses, seemingly the work of an unknown genius. In fact, they had been concocted by two conservative academics, who had "opened books at random" and chosen "a word or a phrase haphazardly."[49] The verses were haphazard phrases - the readers had discovered the meaning, not the authors.

We, too, might randomly select words, and imagine how their intersection might solve our puzzle. For example, how could the words 'fish,' 'mooring,' 'Tasmania,' and 'insoluble' suggest a way of reducing global warming? I chose these words at random, but if you try, you *will* find a way. Our brain is remarkably good at 'making sense' of unexpected connections.

But there is more. We could think in stages. Poincaré suggested that discovery in science and mathematics naturally proceeds systematically - he said that researchers identify a problem in the "preparation" stage, subconsciously consider it during "incubation," intuit a solution via "illumination," and assess the answer in a final phase of "verification."[50] We could follow such staging deliberately, as others have. Walt Disney invented by allocating three mindsets to different rooms of his house, those of 'Dreamer,' 'Realist,' and 'Critic.' He would progressively move from one place to the next, and apply the appropriate mindset in each.[51]

But we don't *require* a particular approach to make a discovery. Launching an investigation may be enough, for we also stumble on findings by chance. The Curies discovered radium when trying to obtain uranium from pitchblende: a high level of radioactivity meant another substance must be present. It was luck, or what scientists call 'serendipity.'[52] Similarly, Michael Faraday discovered the way that magnetism can generate electric current through simple perseverance - he tried again and again, and eventually he made a breakthrough.[53]

And, for some, there is unusual talent. A few people generate answers because they possess exceptional genetic traits. The T/T genotype of the neuregulin one gene is associated with high creative-thinking scores (as well as bipolar disorder and schizophrenia), while Einstein's autopsy found he had an uncommonly large number of glial cells in a brain area associated with imagery (backing his view that his inventiveness came from skill in spatial reasoning).[54] There is a more general effect as well: creativity seems to increase with intelligence, up to an IQ of around 120.[55]

Feelings help find solutions too

Ideas help us make sense of the material world, usually ending as narratives that 'explain' what we see. But skill at identifying and mapping relationships is not the only capacity we use to understand the world. Feelings help too.

Emotions tell us the events that require our conscious attention, although the appropriate event/emotion connection will have to be learned. For example, I remember driving to my granddaughter's birthday party when I felt a sudden, alarming shock!! An instant later, I realized I had not bought her a present.

These alerts can be vital for survival, often signaling from our unconscious, which seems to monitor what is going on around us.[56] A nurse will suddenly fear that a child's health has become worse, or a fire-fighter that a building may collapse; we attend to these signals and remember them. A professional cave diver said, "if you're not afraid now and then, you'd be dead a long time ago."[57]

Feelings also let us know when we have found a solution, or are close to it. Regarding one discovery, Richard Feynman said, "there was a moment when I knew how nature worked," the idea was so elegant and beautiful, "the goddamn thing was gleaming" (concerning the physics of 'weak interactions').[58]

I have had a similar though lesser experience. I was chatting to my Ph.D. supervisor, Ken Forster, when I felt a powerful bodily sensation, like a submarine pushing up through pack ice, followed by an idea for distinguishing the better of two theories, a clue that gave me the basis for my thesis.[59] I have felt signals at a more humdrum level, too - a pulse of excitement when reading an article, followed by a sudden understanding.

Intriguingly, I have also found that one can use emotions to *intentionally* evaluate ideas - I have let a proposition hang in my awareness, waiting to see if it produced good or bad-feelings, a sort of 'feelings-tested reasoning.' The hard work is done unconsciously, but feelings give the advice.

And emotions *motivate* us to find answers. Einstein said his "play with elements" was encouraged by "the desire" to arrive at logically connected concepts[60]. Feelings can give us the drive to persevere until we succeed. The mathematical scientist G.B. Dantzig showed this; when a student, he came late to statistician Jerzy Neyman's class at Berkeley, and found what he thought was mandatory homework on the blackboard; the result was he explained two previously intractable mathematical problems. Later he said you should believe a problem can be solved, and have the conviction you can do it.[61]

Self-belief is essential if your idea is controversial. This was the case with Alfred Wegener, when developing the theory of continental drift. Trained as a meteorologist, not a geologist, Wegener imagined continents moving through ocean floors, "like icebergs through water." He saw that the opposite coastlines of the Atlantic had complementary shapes, and considered data from paleontology and meteorology that others rejected. Mainstream geologists opposed him, but he persisted. Now his theory is entirely accepted.[62] One mathematician argued you should develop ideas alone, for if you read the literature first, "you will be diverted into the train of thought of the other author, and stop exactly where he ran into an obstacle."[63]

Feelings have been under-recognized

Probably more should be added regarding emotion and reasoning, but for much of its life, cognitive psychology has ignored feelings (although this may be changing, given evidence, which we will later encounter, that emotion plays a crucial role in personal choices).

We have learned other things about feelings. For example, emotional responses change with age - past the age of sixty, we are more likely to cry in movies.[64] And we can have several feelings at once; in a US study of college students, one told how a lecturer had made a joke and no one laughed, and the observing student was both amused and sorry at the same time.[65] On the other hand, we don't know how many different types of feelings there are, although there seems to be a large number. When I witness Tchaikovsky's Swan Lake, I experience many complex inner sensations, each of which I could label a *'feeling'* (an artwork, too, can provoke diverse emotions, many of which are hard to describe).

Given the close relationship between emotional feelings and physical sensations, there could be as many emotions as we have states of brain and body.

We sometimes make mistakes

We will decide more wisely if we know how the material world works. However, understanding its mechanisms is not enough, for human factors interfere with our ability to see the world. If we are to learn to decide appropriately, we need to be on the alert for these factors. I review some of them in the following.

Processing is limited

One source of mistakes is our limited capacity to process information. In a well-known experiment, observers had to count passes between basketball teams – the task was highly demanding, and they failed to see a costumed 'gorilla' walk between the players.[66] Processing limits and task demands mean we often fail to analyze correctly. Shanteau conducted a review, and concluded that stockbrokers, clinical psychologists, psychiatrists, college admissions officers, court judges, personnel selectors, and intelligence analysts, all regularly miss the mark. On the other hand, he felt livestock judges, astronomers, test pilots, soil judges, chess masters, physicists, mathematicians, accountants, grain inspectors, photo interpreters, and insurance analysts usually can meet a suitable standard. Less clear was the ability of nurses, physicians, and auditors. Shanteau thought they were somewhere in the middle.[67]

We forget but think we know

A second source of error is memory shortcomings. For example, we are good at remembering emotional events, but we fail to recall what else was happening. This was shown when the U.S. space shuttle Challenger was lost. People were asked what they were doing when they heard the news, and queried again two and a half years later. Those remembering had high confidence in their answers, but their two reports disagreed dramatically.[68] Our memory fails in the short term too. Patients receiving bad news, like a diagnosis of cancer, often can't remember the advice regarding treatment provided at the same time - it needs to be given again and again.[69]

Memory problems are made worse by our tendency to make up explanations, that is, to 'confabulate.' When people were asked to select the most attractive of a set of faces, but had their choices covertly switched, they still gave reasons why they made their supposed 'choice' (the one they didn't make).[70] If needed, we create entirely new memories.

Disneyland visitors shown a fake advertisement for Bugs Bunny reported seeing him, although he couldn't have been there (he is not a Disney character).[71] Unfortunately, manufactured memories can seem as real as true ones, which can mean bad news for those in a court case and relying on accurate recall from witnesses.

We see what we expect

A third type of error occurs when what we have just seen or experienced leads us to mistakenly recognize what follows, or be biased in how we interpret it. This is called 'priming.' Priming helps us perceive events, but it can also mean we misrecognize or understand in a prejudiced way.

I remember I had attended a travel writing course – I was dreaming of being a freelance writer – when on the bus home, I suddenly heard a young boy say, "Safari Park." On attending to this exciting conversation, I discovered he had said, "Ferris wheel" (we had just passed one). My thoughts on travel writing had led me to mishear his words.

Another blatant misperception was when I saw a beautiful woman seated in a parked car near my home. My heart raced. I avoided eye contact, but as I walked by, I could not resist a quick, shy glance at her face. What I saw was a heavily beaded rug covering the top of an empty seat, of the type sometimes used by people with back or neck problems. That was all; the beads gave intense colors and visual contour, but there had never been a beautiful woman. My attraction to beautiful women (and the beads) was enough for me to see one.

Priming also changes how we interpret. When people were given a crime report, and asked what to do, the advice they offered depended on the words used in the preamble. If crime was called a "virus," they proposed prevention. If crime was described as a "beast," they advocated harsher laws.[72] Similarly, priming changed the assessment of those appraising a videoed fight contest - fighters wearing red trunks were given more points than those wearing blue, even though there was no difference in performance (the trunk colors were altered digitally).[73]

The effects of priming words (or events) have long been known. Quintilian, a Roman instructor of public speaking (35-95 A.D), observed that metaphors "lend credibility to our arguments, and steal their way secretly into the minds of the judges."[74]

For this reason, priming is much-used in advertising. For example, pictures of attractive people are used to make the product more desirable, which they do effectively. When male finance customers were given promotional information, they took out more short-term loans if the material included a photo of an attractive woman.[75] In the same way, priming can be treacherous - printing the words "silver" or "gold" on boxes of cigarettes meant smokers judged them to be more healthy.[76]

In general, priming is a useful aid to recognition, particularly if the event is uncommon or degraded, but it can mislead us.

We stick to an idea like a dog to a bone

The final source of errors I will describe is arguably the most severe. Known as "confirmation bias,"[77] it is where we stick to an idea despite clear evidence we are wrong and focus on information supporting our mistaken view.

In medicine, it can mean faulty diagnosis. When physicians were asked to diagnose patients with signs of both cardiac and muscular-skeletal illness, half the doctors based their determinations *only* on the musculoskeletal information. If the disease of these patients had been cardiac, the consequences could have been fatal.[78]

Regrettably, a one-eyed approach is standard - we all defend favored positions. As put by William James, "we carve out order by leaving the disorderly parts out."[79]

Politicians and lawyers make their living by focusing on only one side of an argument. Scientists do it too. Intelligent and well-informed researchers passionately guard their favored propositions, while equally capable and informed researchers vigorously assert the opposite. In the 1970s and 1980s, rival camps of researchers in cognitive psychology defended different models for how word meanings are organized, the 'logogen' versus 'search' models.[80] The proponents of each theory read the same literature but maintained opposing positions (I know because I was one of them).

Sometimes our biased view is supported by an emotional reaction. Physician Jerome Groopman described how a smelly, unshaven man disgusted his examining doctor, who diagnosed him as an alcoholic when the patient suffered from "Wilson's disease," a condition that mimics chronic drunkenness.[81]

And when multiple people are involved, things become worse. One individual follows another, and the mistake becomes entrenched. This, too, occurs in medicine. Writing a provisional interpretation on an x-ray envelope can influence the radiologist's analysis of the film, potentially supporting a faulty diagnosis; this is known as "diagnosis momentum" (clinical interpretation should wait until the radiologist has examined the film).[82]

Various laboratory settings have been used to investigate confirmation bias. In one, people acted as 'divorce judges' – they had to decide which of two parents should receive custody of a child. One parent was described with negative and positive attributes, and the other blandly. Remarkably, whether asked for the best or worst parent, the judges always selected the same person - the one with the rich, detailed description. It seems that once the target attributes are defined, only those features are used to make a choice.[83]

"Hindsight bias"[84] is a related form of biased judgment. When a linkage has been demonstrated, the relationship becomes self-evident. Again, this has been shown in medical practice. Once physicians were told which diagnosis was the right one, they became sure it was apparent from the beginning.[85] The paleontologist Stephen Jay Gould gave another illustration. He said, "People tend to look at world history and prehistory and claim certain events - like the emergence of human beings - were inevitable and predictable ... [but] much of the 'patterning' we see is ... a clumping of results within a random system."[86]

Why do we have confirmation bias and hindsight bias? Perhaps because they make us respond decisively. Confirmation bias means we adopt an explanation and proceed - we don't swing between conflicting accounts and opposing courses of action. Similarly, hindsight bias will reduce uncertainty, allowing us to make immediate use of our new understanding. This certainty could have helped us survive - doubting or hesitating would have been fatal in lethal combat, or when stalked by a big cat. Instead of questioning, we acted.

However, leaping into action has less value in modern life. Now, we have more time to think, and in most activities, accuracy is better than speed. The physician Jerome Groopman observed that "studied calm" is advisable even in a hospital's emergency department, that staff must always fully consider the implications of the patient's symptoms.[87]

Fortunately, we can reduce our commitment to just one view. Neuro-psychologists were less likely to overstate the likelihood of a diagnosis (they were given a case history and the correct diagnosis) if they also had to state why the finding could have been two other conditions.[88] It seems that if we make a case for alternatives, our view will be more supple.

Confirmation and hindsight bias hinder the right choice - they maintain false conclusions. We need to reject the business man's dictum, "there is no such thing as a bad decision," and substitute the adage, "always be ready to see a better way." We have to incorporate new information, and be ready to change our minds.

We have found a way to reason well

It is clear we need a culture of examination, not one of seizing to an answer. Fortunately, we already have it. After many centuries of development, questioning is now part of the greatest collaborative achievement of humankind. We call it science, or more accurately, "the scientific method."

Science is an extraordinary tool for circumventing biases. It has succeeded spectacularly. It has meant heart surgery, the internet, space travel, and could probably tell us how to restore our environment (if given the opportunity).

Why does science succeed? It is not due to the way scientists intuit ideas - they generate potential answers in much the same way as other people do. But in science, after thousands of years of thought and argument in natural philosophy, hypotheses must be based on *observation*. In 1662 the British Royal Society asked seamen traveling the world to "put aside what others have written" and look at nature to form "a solid and useful philosophy."[89] Later Sir

Isaac Newton (president of the Royal Society) famously explained the path of a falling apple with an account of gravity based on observation and measurement - the inverse square law.[90]

And there is a second principle. Having gathered data and theorized, scientists must *test* the ideas. Testing is as vital as conceiving the hypothesis in the first place; checking is exhaustive, comprehensive, and continuing. It is why scientific research is often described as 'one part inspiration and nine parts perspiration.'

This examination is commonly guided by the "hypothetico-deductive" method, associated with the philosopher of science, Karl Popper. The method proposes that one forms a theory and makes predictions based on that theory, then gathers and examines data relating to the forecasts. If the predictions are confirmed, the theory is supported; if they are not endorsed, the argument is rejected.[91]

The primacy of testing is an extraordinary boon. It means ideas can be considered even if they are unorthodox, outlandish, or even absurd. The method of science causes the right notions to be supported, and the false ones discarded. The wheat is separated from the chaff.

How is such testing conducted? There are various ways to validly and reliably test a hypothesis or proposal. In the biological and medical sciences, the most respected method (or experimental design) is the double-blind, randomized controlled trial, or RCT. The RCT may, for example, be used to assess the relationship between drug treatment and improvement in a patient's condition. It involves researchers varying a 'treatment' such as the dose of a particular drug (the 'independent variable') while observing its 'effect' on an outcome measure such as the patient's reported pain (the 'dependent variable'). Patients are randomly allocated varying amounts of the drug, and clinicians and patients are kept oblivious ('blinded') to the dosage each patient receives. As neither patients nor clinicians know how much medication is administered - only the researcher knows – then the observed effects can be attributed to the drug treatment. Hence the name 'double-blind, randomized controlled trial.'

There are further principles that are part of science. A key one is that prestige, authority, and ideology means naught: all ideas are to be questioned, and all propositions are to be assessed based solely on the data. The advent of relativity theory and quantum mechanics showed this was needed; unlike what had been thought, Newton had not solved all the big questions[92] (this rejection of authority stands in sharp contrast to what happens in politics, as will be discussed in the next chapter).

Another guiding idea is 'parsimony.' When forming a theory, the simplest possible explanation is preferred (also known as 'Occam's razor').[93] An example is Darwin's and Wallace's theory of evolution, which explained the diversity of species based on only a few propositions.

There is, however, a worm in the science apple. As already noted, individual scientists may adhere to out-lived theories, but there is worse - some intentionally mislead.

In a confidential 2005 survey, one in three US healthcare researchers reported engaging in at least one unethical behavior in the previous three years. The ways included ignoring data opposing one's research, excluding data based on 'gut feeling,' or changing a research report to please a benefactor. Similar behaviors appeared in a 2012 study, which attempted to confirm the results of fifty-seven "landmark" oncology drug trials; in only 10% could the findings be confirmed. It seems that scientists apply less scrutiny when their findings support their interests.[94]

Fortunately, though, there is also good news. While individual researchers may pursue favored explanations, and some may even rig the data to support their preferred discoveries, science 'the enterprise' is neither partisan nor self-interested. Typically, ideas are tested by opposing research camps, and the better theory will eventually triumph. Hence Wallace and Darwin's theory of natural selection (based on survival of the fittest) was opposed for decades but was finally accepted. And Wegener's theory of continental drift was in time adopted, although it initially met high resistance.

Science fosters unfettered competition, with different parties promoting the value of their unique views, and all proposals tested. Incorrect explanations are not entrenched, better answers are found, and the result is an ever-expanding base of scientific knowledge and technique. In this way, science has mostly overcome the problem of confirmation bias. Its method for understanding the mechanisms of the world is valid, whatever the policy aim or field of investigation.

Science must be understood and applied

However, discovering answers is not enough - society has to make use of them. We have to learn from scientific findings and change our views and attitudes in line with the evidence. In this respect, John Maynard Keynes was reportedly asked about a switch in his thinking; he is said to have replied, "When my information changes, I change my mind. What do you do, Sir?"

To ensure the best policies, researchers and politicians must work together. Collaboration does occur, both routinely and when emergencies require a particular focus - the COVID 19 pandemic is an example. But it is not always the case. In the crisis of global warming, collaboration has been lacking. Scientists have warned of progressively chaotic and dangerous weather, pointing both to historical data and recent events - extreme storms, droughts, fires, and floods. Yet many politicians have preferred their interpretations, such as, "it's normal." Such a position is unacceptable. When our environment, even our survival, is at risk, science *must* guide our decisions.

Being guided by scientific evidence is an obligation we have to our grandchildren.

Summary: examine the science

The physical world, the world of things, lies all around us. We seek to identify its mechanisms by observing, aided by imagination, metaphor, and mathematics; and following many years of development, by science.

Science takes our insights and subjects them to exhaustive testing, and so explains the material world. It does not kowtow to personal interests - it is based on observed relationships and likelihood. With science, we describe, predict, and find solutions.

How well has humanity performed in understanding the material world? It's hard to judge how much of what can be known *is* known, but through science, our knowledge has increased dramatically and continues to grow. Maybe if we had to give ourselves a mark for understanding the material world, it would be, say, seven out of ten?

Yet humans are flawed - we identify in error, overlook what is critical, and persist with opinions contradicted by the data. If we are to improve, we must all understand the basics of science and base our decisions upon it. We need to become *'questioning world thinkers.'*

What does this entail?

A questioning world thinker -

- Appreciates how science works
- Makes decisions based on the data
- Looks out for mistakes in what is observed
- Encourages new ideas, aware that current ones can be wrong
- Changes her view in line with the evidence
- Elects leaders that pay attention to science

We have investigated the first domain of thinking, the material world; there are three to go. We will find that not all have progressed as well.

CHAPTER 2.

Knowing People By
Seeing Ourselves

Contained within the realm of things, equally important, wonderfully complex, and representing more to us than anything, is a second domain – the world of *people*. People are the most vital part of our lives. In a 1969 popular song, a child is struggling to carry a younger little boy, and someone asks if he is not too heavy. The carrying child replies, "No, he's not heavy... he's my brother." I have heard that line a hundred times, yet it still brings a lump to my throat.[95]

We rely on our kind; we need each other. Refugees surveyed by Amnesty International Australia said they were less anxious when they knew someone cared; they didn't feel alone.[96] In life and death situations, we provide mutual support. Halina Birenbaum told of being a teenager in a Nazi death camp, where there was also a boy she loved. Halina said she did not feel bad when escorted by the SS through Auschwitz, as she could "feel Abram's loving gaze upon me, the touch of his hand, his kisses on my face."[97] In ordinary times, we gain backing too. I remember being anxious before my first overseas project, but then an acquaintance told me she believed in me, and almost immediately, my confidence returned.

We sense others feelings

From the beginning, we sense and respond to people. Babies feel what other babies are feeling, and cry when they hear them crying; it is called 'emotion contagion.'[98] Babies also comfort and protect each other. Bloom observed, "if they [babies] see someone suffer, even silently, they become distressed. And as soon as they can move, babies will try to help. They'll stroke the person, or hand over a toy or bottle."[99] Babies also recognize goodness and kindness. Hamlin and co-workers presented infants with a puppet play - a character would struggle up a hill, one puppet would help, another would push him down. When later presented with the dolls, children as young as six months would reach for 'the good one.'[100]

As our early responsiveness shows, we don't need language to communicate. We can tell what people are thinking from facial expression, touch, gesture, movements, and odor. As adults, we use non-verbal information to estimate "attractiveness, trust-worthiness, competence, and aggression" within half a second of seeing another's face.[101] And tone of voice: the neurologist Oliver Sachs described how people with severe aphasia, those for whom words have no meaning, understand others based on the sounds of their voices.[102]

And we may have discovered the neural processes that allow us to do it.

Reading minds with how *we* feel

In the early 1990s, Rizzolatti, Fogassi, and Gallese at the University of Parma were studying the motor cortex of a macaque monkey when they discovered a group of nerve cells that fired when the macaque took hold of a banana. Then, they noticed that the same nerves fired when *the monkey saw one of the experimenters* pick up a banana. A group of neurons was active both when the monkey ate a banana, and when it watched a researcher do the same. They called them "mirror neurons."[103]

These cells have since been identified in humans. They become active both when we act, and when we see another person (or creature) perform in the same way. For example, there are cells that fire when we smile, and also when we see someone else smile[104] - which explains how seeing someone smile makes us feel like smiling too.

Mirror neurons are vehicles for 'automatic empathy.' These remarkable brain cells allow us to experience what it's like to be in another's situation, and to guess their thoughts, feelings, and perceptions - that is, if we have previously had the same experience. Before mirror neurons, we broadly assumed we use reasoning to understand and predict other's actions. Now it is likely we know people by a spontaneous activation of counterpart feelings and thoughts, a knowledge by simulation.

It seems feelings, as well as reasoning, can tell us what another could be thinking.

Mirror neurons may help us do more than read minds. They might explain why we imitate the actions of other people, such as their posture, facial expressions, and gestures,[105] and, at a more general level, how it is that humans and other primates learn skills from each other. They could have even given rise to language.[106]

By their existence, mirror neurons have legitimized a different metaphor for explaining people. In place of 'humans who are wise,' we can be described as 'humans who understand others through their feelings.'

We mind-read other creatures

Whatever the details of the underlying mechanism, our 'reading the minds' of others is remarkably general. For example, we imagine the feelings and thoughts of non-living things. When shown geometric shapes moving around a box, people described the actions in social terms, like "the circle is chasing the triangle."[107]

And we empathize with other species. I remember seeing a tortoise crossing a road towards a lake. My knowledge of tortoise habits is slight, but I immediately sensed the lake was the tortoise's goal. I felt the sensations it would receive when entering the water, the coolness from immersion, and the reduced weight of its shell. I also worried it might be run-over before it completed its journey.

Other animals may empathize as we do. They may use mirror neurons to understand each other, and 'read the minds' of people. After all, our knowledge of mirror neurons started with macaques.

We read minds by trusting others

Mirror neurons are a mechanism for sensing what people are feeling and thinking, centered on how they appear. Do we understand others based on how they present to us?

The answer seems to be yes. For we judge people based on appearances even if told we are being misled.

This was shown when American students debated pro- and anti-Castro positions. Observers were told the stances of the debaters were randomly assigned, yet they still felt the debaters' views reflected their genuine convictions - seeing a debater argue for Castro made them think the debater was *a real* Castro supporter.[108] The same was found in a study simulating a quiz show. Again onlookers were told the roles were randomly assigned, yet they none the less considered the "quizmasters" to be more intelligent than the "contestants." It seems we are hard-wired to understand others based on the way they look.

There are advantages to judging others based on how they seem and what they do, which are beautifully illustrated by the honeybee. When bees need a new nesting site, many bees fly out to search. On their return, they perform a "waggle dance," which tells the other bees where they have been and how good a nest-site they have found. The watching bees judge the quality of each prospective nesting place based on the intensity of each searcher's dance and use it to choose a new site. This remarkable collaboration requires that the performers honestly and accurately represent each possible location, which they do. The result is the hive gains the best place, and maximizes the common good.[109]

Trust offers similar rewards to humans, that is, if we are trustworthy. By being honest, we can exchange information and learn from each other. Fortunately, we generally are, we cooperate even when it costs us.[110]

There is a further benefit from believing others. It means we will believe 'a good lie,' a proposition that will strengthen us. In Tolstoy's *War and Peace*, the Russian general Kutuzov explained that lies could be valuable, that appearing self-assured before his troops was essential for their morale and eventual victory. Churchill knew this too, when he rallied his nation with portentous tones, telling them, "we shall never surrender." And doctors may help their patients withstand serious illness, by confidently advising, "Yes, there is hope."

Trust based on appearances may also explain why we follow those with great self-belief. By watching a charismatic person, we will sense what they appear to feel, and projecting this back, we will trust them. A business partner of mine had such a manner: he radiated confidence. I remember watching the expression on people's faces as he entered a room. He was smiling broadly, and almost immediately, so were most of those present. His warmth induced the same state in the watchers. They lit up. They just wanted to touch him.[111]

Trust is a mixed blessing

Trust lets us mind-read, receive support from 'white lies,' share information, and follow those with self-belief. But lying with a straight face is not confined to earnest leaders or philosopher-kings; 'appearing' is not the same as 'being.'

Indeed, some pretenders are *all* pretense, assuming a false appearance to gain at our expense. And on meeting these, we will believe them – we will trust the conman and be duped. As one confidence trickster admitted, "The thing about people is that they want to believe you, you don't have to give them much, and they'll come right along."[112]

We will take bare-faced liars at face value, which can be a problem, particularly if they are a leader. A poised manner and self-assured tone of voice may have wrongly decided many elections.

Factors that affect empathy

While we take people at face value, we trust some people more than others. So what is needed for us to feel empathy and sympathy?

We feel most insight and caring when people are similar to us and have had related experiences. I once heard a dedicated Elvis Presley fan and impersonator, say, "wherever I go, all over the world, I meet people I feel I have known all my life." That is, when he met other Elvis Presley impersonators. And we identify with characters in a novel if they are like us; it is called 'narrative transport.'

We also feel more understanding if we like how the other person behaves. For example, if in a relationship crisis, they express sadness, not anger. Or, if unwell, they are not responsible for their state, suffering from cancer, say, as opposed to drug addiction.[113]

Knowing personal details helps us empathize, as demonstrated by aid appeals. People make substantial contributions if the money is to go to, "Rokia, a 7-year-old girl from Mali, Africa, desperately poor, and facing a threat of severe hunger and starvation", but are much less generous if the money is "to reduce the hunger of twenty-one million people in Malawi, Zambia, Angola, and Ethiopia."[114] Seeing a person's face encourages caring too. In one study, people gave five times more money if shown a photo of the person they were asked to help.[115]

Gender also makes a difference: females are more empathic than males. In the 'reading the mind in the eyes' test, people were shown photos of eyes and asked to identify the person's feelings and thoughts - women were significantly better at this than men. This gender difference seems to begin early; female children show more sympathy than boys, even when toddlers[116].

Why are females more sympathetic and caring? It could partly be due to upbringing, but hormones also play a part. Oxytocin promotes social behavior and is higher in females, while testosterone reduces trust and is higher in males.

Taking these factors together, one might say that you will be understood by one who is female, similar to you, likes you, and knows your details. On the other hand, you are likely to be mistrusted if the person is male, different from you, dislikes you, and knows little about you.

If there is no empathy, you may be harmed, as revealed in healthcare. In a 2004 Swiss survey, Escher et al. found that patients with a pleasant personality were more likely to be admitted to intensive care, while in a 2007 study, Greer and others discovered that U.S. doctors gave suboptimal treatment if the patient was black.[117]

Overall, our ability to work effectively with others seems to be governed by those factors that direct empathy and trust. Being similar could be the biggest - if we feel alike (accurately or mistakenly), we are likely to trust and collaborate. If we feel no kinship, we can be detached and adversarial.

Working with groups and leaders

We have considered how empathy and trust are developed and guide the way we relate to other people. Similar factors guide another social behavior – following.

Our need to follow

As a graduate student, I remember watching the gestures and smiles of the academic staff in the Department of Psychology at Monash University in Australia as they displayed their knowledge of white wine, chardonnay versus riesling. Their behaviors were indistinguishable from those of American and Australian hippies I had seen in Kabul, showing off their knowledge of hashish, 'Bombay Black' versus 'Afghani Brown.' In both groups, individual members paraded and adjusted their views to gain approval.

We are all influenced by groups whose members are akin to us, or groups we wish to be part of; we mimic and seek to join them. But the consequences of such linkages are not always benign. The Framingham Heart Study followed 4000 people for twenty years and found that whether a person smoked or not depended on the habits of their spouse, friends, coworkers, and siblings – an individual's smoking behavior could be predicted from the customs of others.[118]

Sometimes we copy behaviors that are obviously dangerous. I remember waiting to cross a busy road guarded by traffic lights. There was a large group of us, and suddenly a person darted across against the lights. Then several more - and suddenly, all those waiting found themselves moving as one. And the last few (including me) were almost run down, for as we left the curb, a car came speeding around the corner and was upon us.

This group behavior was accidental, but groups can *intend* to exert pressure, to support the views of the majority. For groups dislike dissenters, they ignore uncommon ideas and suppress innovative ones even in brainstorming groups. In 1991 Mullen et al. found that when groups aim to generate ideas, they produce less than when the individuals are asked separately.

Suppression of personal views occurs in the laboratory too. Asch found that when people were asked to select the longest of several bars, they would ignore what they see to follow a group.[119] And we follow in politics. Cohen found that peoples' attitudes to social issues changes in step with the policies of their political party, even when the policies contradict their personal values.[120] It is not easy to be a dissenter when the group has a different view.

And this introduces a potentially worse form of lemming-like behavior. Numerous studies have revealed we recklessly follow the dictates of our leaders or seniors (those in more elevated positions). For example, people administered electric shocks to innocent subjects when required by a white-coated researcher.[121] Others accepted poor financial advice, when an "expert" gave it.[122] And in real-life, deference to leaders can mean lives are lost.

In *Into Thin Air,* a brave account by Jon Krakauer of a 1996 climbing attempt on Mount Everest, the author describes how he agreed he should follow the expedition head (who was his friend). The outcome was he did not try to over-rule the leader when he showed signs of hypoxia and directed the group to push on to the summit under hostile weather conditions. Because Jon failed to speak up, his friend died.[123]

Following seniors has meant lost-lives in healthcare too. The Bristol Hospital scandal in the UK revealed years of poor performance by senior surgeons. While lower-ranking staff were fully aware of their seniors' incompetence, they were over-awed and failed to speak out.[124] And in an Australian hospital, nurses and junior doctors failed to call medical emergency teams when needed, because of fear of senior doctors.[125]

On speaking up

Our leaders don't always act appropriately, but we make matters worse if we go along with them. We need to change and adopt the principle used in science – follow the evidence, not the person. When we see wrong behavior, we need to support our consciences and speak up.

Fearless independent voices are as needed today as they were two thousand years ago. From 300 BC to 500 AD, the Greco-Roman elite administered their great multi-ethnic societies under the dominant philosophy of Stoicism. Marcus Aurelius, Roman emperor in the second century BCE and stoic philosopher, espoused action unaffected by greed or fear - he believed all should say and do what they believe is right. He set out his views in *Meditations,* writings still admired today.[126]

Societies need people with independent minds. They guide leaders, and result in more ideas and more answers. Senor and Singer described how the Israeli military accepted that a good idea could come from anyone at any time. "If you're a junior officer, you call your higher-ups by their first names, and if you see them doing something wrong, you say so." Speaking up means higher productivity, and may explain why there were more Israeli technology organizations listed on Nasdaq in 2009 than any country except the USA.[127]

Opinions, expressed fearlessly, also produce a safer environment. This has been recognized in aviation.

Following a history of accidents due to human error, the aviation industry now advocates shared problem-solving, coupled with graded assertiveness: if a member of a flight crew thinks there is a problem, then s/he must raise the issue, initially gently, but with increasing insistence. Even the most junior is to speak up if they see a dangerous situation, and the chief officer has to listen.[128]

In healthcare, too, attempts are being made to create a flatter, less hierarchical structure, where whistleblowing is encouraged.[129]

Every organization needs individuals to report dangerous, unethical, improper, or illegal actions. We must not kowtow to our seniors; we all have to speak up. We help all of us when we do.

Choosing a leader

As well as standing up to leaders, we have to pick the right ones. These choices are critical, for once chosen, we are likely to follow these individuals (even when they violate our beliefs).

First, let's consider who *not* to select. Someone overflowing with self-belief is not automatically a prime candidate - self-confidence is a characteristic of champions, but it is also of charlatans. A propensity for swift and assertive action is unwanted, too; decisiveness is hazardous, even in a hospital emergency department. Perhaps the achievement of prior high position is a sound indicator? No, because expertise in one area does not mean skill in another. And one should rarely choose the demagogue or 'dog whistler' – a person willing to excite gut-responses may quickly abandon ethics.

Does this suggest we sometimes elect people based on characteristics unrelated to their suitability as a leader? Quite likely.

Who will be a good leader? Such a person will favor research - we want policies based on evidence. A 'worrier' is also suitable; they will produce more considered judgments. And a good leader will believe in flexibility; they will not refuse to change for fear of seeming to 'flip-flop.' Their mantra will be 'change when the evidence requires it.'

Based on the evidence, the best leader is likely to be female. Women are more open to diverse inputs, more likely to consider others, and they work better in groups to solve problems.[130] Empathy studies suggest women are also more likely to be kind, a valuable quality, according to Xuanzang, a 6th Century Chinese scholar who visited North India to learn from the original Buddhist scriptures. He judged Indian leaders based on this last standard, believing it to be one of the most valuable qualities a leader could possess.[131]

And a 2020 Australian study found that women make better CEOs. Organizations were more successful when a woman was appointed to leadership, a female CEO increasing market value by an average of 5 percent ($80 million for an ASX200 company). The same study found female CEOs were more democratic, more collaborative, less corrupt, and possessed a greater sense of corporate social responsibility.[132]

Selecting the right leader is critically important. At the national level, the right leader will save us, her people, and the wrong one can destroy us. Our leaders have *huge* responsibilities. Most of all, they must put the nation's interests before their own.

Understand intentionally

Empathy and trust have produced complex, thriving societies. Yet some individuals, groups, and leaders intend to deceive us for their gain, which means that blind faith in others will hurt us. If so, how can we retain the benefits of trust, while avoiding the costs of being deceived?

I suggest *caveat emptor* ('let the buyer beware') - to understand a person or a group, we need to research them.

We do this when considering a new event, such as childbirth or skydiving. We investigate, and then form the encounter in our imagination (we will later refer to this mental representation as a 'scenario'). We may ask our friends if they have had the experience and if they enjoyed it. We take steps to learn about it and imagine what it could be like.

In much the same way, we can inquire into people's lives. If we know their history, experiences, hopes, and memories, we can place ourselves in their circumstances. Then they will become more familiar, more accessible, more like us. We will understand people based on what we discover, not rely on our immediate reactions.

For, as I said before, our spontaneous reactions can be misleading. If people are different, if we lack shared characteristics, we may feel little or no empathy. If another person is weirdly-dressed and strange-acting - perhaps they are from a different culture – we will likely withdraw from them. For example, we will find a scene of marching, self-flagellating men incomprehensible unless we have been educated in Shiite history and belief.[133]

We can develop informed empathy, even when communities are currently in conflict. In 2004, the Israeli Minister of Justice Yosef Lapid questioned the practice of demolishing Palestinian houses. He did so after seeing an old woman on her knees in her ruined home, looking for her medicines. He said, "What would I say if it were my grandmother?"[134]

Actively educating ourselves, becoming acquainted with others' situations, views, and experiences, and *then* feeling how they feel, will produce a better informed 'being in the other's shoes.' Intentionally developing empathy may "rid us of the curse of xenophobia," as the primatologist Frans de Waal described it.[135]

And we will better appreciate how others may react. George Saville (1633-1695), 1st Marquess of Halifax and English statesman, observed: "Could we know what men are most apt to remember, we might know what they are most apt to do."[136]

Forming a deeper acquaintance with those we are unfamiliar with will mean fewer surprises and less over-reactions, both from them and from us. This lessening of division will benefit us all.

Summary: understand by inquiry, not gut

People need people. But to cooperate, we have to feel we will get on, and we assess based on appearances. If the person seems to be like us, we trust them and cooperate; if the person appears different, we may not.

We use impressions to guide us in the groups we identify with, the leaders we select, and our attitudes to whole communities. We don't conduct research - as science would advise – we go on first impressions.

Selecting a poor leader may be the most conspicuous failure of this process. We go with our gut and then stick to our choice, even if the person later contradicts our values.

We stay with our attitudes to other cultures too – it can be in our interest to overcome our differences, but instead, we retreat and confirm our opposing position.

What can we do about this poor method of favoring and rejecting people? We need to constrain automatic empathy, and pursue 'intentional learning' - to research others, not rely on spontaneous judgments. In this way, we can find commonalities. When the matter is critical, we need to engage, so our nature does not shunt us into closed, destructive paths. This applies to individuals, groups, cultures, and leaders

Worldwide, we have made some progress. We have formed trans-cultural organizations to regulate and protect actions between nations (such as the United Nations, the World Health Organization, and the International Court of Justice), and nations have constitutions, democratic processes, and ways to regulate unruly officials. We also have codes of ethics, laws, and caring institutions.

However, instead of science, we have horse-trading, better known as politics. We need an 'Applied Science of Humans,' a technology for making decisions based on the pooled know-how of social psychology, anthropology, and primatology, one that provides practical advice on avoiding pitfalls and adopting new opportunities.

The realm of people is challenging. When it comes to understanding each other, I suggest we score six out of ten. However, some individuals *are* good at it; appearances do not dictate to them. They reconnoiter the person, their feelings, memories, and beliefs. I will call this individual, one skilled in people thinking, an *'inquiring mind reader.'*

An inquiring mind reader -

- Intentionally learns other people's feelings and experiences before they act or judge. They don't rely on their intuitive reactions.
- Forms their own views and ideas, instead of copying others
- Questions, and gives feedback, to all
- Elects leaders based on a comprehensive investigation of the candidate's qualities, not gut-feeling
- Wants at least fifty percent of high-level decision-makers to be female.

CHAPTER 3.

Finding Happiness
Via Time Travel

We wrestle with the worlds of things and people, but what we want is happiness. In western societies, happiness is praised from childhood - my mother often said this was all she wanted for me. We desire pleasure and contentment, and we plan, predict, and choose to achieve that. We do this in our third thinking domain - the world of our inner self.

In search of good feelings

We succeed in being happy, partly because of our genes. Studies of twins have shown that forty to sixty percent of our happiness is genetically determined.[137] Happiness or 'satisfaction with life' is changed by life events, particularly big ones like marriage, unemployment, births, and deaths, but it usually comes back to its former level. And it alters with age – we are least satisfied in our late forties – but happiness returns as we age further.[138]

We try to be happy. David Hume pointed this out in 1777. He said, "the ultimate ends of human actions... recommend themselves entirely to the sentiments and affections of mankind,"[139] which means we do what gives us pleasure or enjoyment. More recently (in 1980), Zajonc observed, "I decided in favor of X," means no more than, "I liked X."[140] In other words, our feelings direct our choices.

Neurologist Anton Damasio provided strong evidence that feelings guide decisions in his 1994 book, "Descarte's Error." Damasio described patients with injuries to the prefrontal cortex, part of the brain involved in emotion. They had average intelligence, memory, and logical thought, yet they could not make up their minds. Instead, they 'endlessly pondered pros and cons,' and when they did decide, their choices were poor. Lacking any feelings associated with situations or actions, they had nothing to direct them.[141]

It seems we use emotion to tell us what to do.

Judging by time travel

To make a personal decision based on feelings, we identify what the options are and judge their consequences. To do this, we form 'scenarios,' imaginary versions of possible futures. Once created, we mentally inhabit them. If we like the feelings evoked, we favor the corresponding decision and action (or not, as appropriate). This mental process is termed 'time-traveling.[142]

For example, I remember my partner asking my thoughts on a revealing dress that she was considering for work. I found myself imagining and feeling different situations. Each time one came to mind, I felt emotional ripples, like stones thrown into a pond. Later, I noted them down.

- I imagined her being at work wearing the dress. *Troubled feelings*
- I thought about what women often wear to work. *Unsure*
- I mentally compared her dress to that I have seen worn by others. *Feelings against*
- I considered her right to wear what she liked. *Feelings in favor of wearing*
- I sensed my feelings if she wore it now. *Feelings against*
- And how I might feel later. *Unsure*

Although they were hypothetical situations, I still felt them – the sensations were milder than would occur in real events, but sufficient to indicate their nature.

They combined to form a judgment: "don't wear it." I wasn't sure how the emotional algebra worked, I never sensed I had worked it out, but 'not wearing' felt more right. I gave my opinion, and my partner said she would tone it down. I was left feeling relieved, and a little guilty.

We conduct this type of imagining-and-feeling every-day. I ask my partner, "Do you want to come to the shops?" and she replies, "Ask me when you're ready, and I will see how I feel." Scenarios let us assess a plan by emotionally experiencing its consequences.

Being (mis)guided by strong feelings

However, time-traveling does not always work well. As it is dependent on feelings, we can be misled by unrelated emotions. When we are already in the grip of strong emotions (like anger, fear, or sexual arousal), our judgment is derailed. We are likely to overreact.

This means that when bad situations arise, they can be followed by unfortunate decisions, as has been observed in politics. Harry Evans, Clerk of the Australian Senate (the upper house of the Australian Federal Parliament) for more than twenty years, recalled on retiring that "the greater the crisis, the more likely politicians will make mistakes in attempting to deal with it."[143] Strong *positive* feelings can mean poor decisions too - in discussing the international financial crisis (GFC), the Noble prize-winning economist Paul Klugman was quoted to say that failures in economic forecasts had occurred because economists "mistook beauty, clad in impressive-looking mathematics, for truth."[144] Laboratory investigations have found similar; for example, one study found that excited feelings encouraged risky investment decisions.[145]

Not only do strong feelings cause us to judge the issue poorly, they can become misguided and target innocent parties. For example, when buoyed up by a concert, we feel warmly towards the strangers sitting beside us. And returning home from work, we find fault with our children, not because of their behavior but due to our workplace mood. Also, far worse – for strong negative emotions can lead to deaths. Historical data shows that economic downturns in 19th Century America led to the scapegoating and murder of many blameless black American people.[146]

In contrast, the Dunedin Study showed the benefits of exercising self-control. Here one thousand children were followed for over forty years, with self-control measured from age three. It was found that greater emotion regulation led to better physical and financial health, less substance abuse, and reduced criminal offending.[147]

If our feelings are tempting us, we will almost certainly be wrong, at least to some degree. *If we feel strongly, we should do nothing!*

We want 'more'

Heightened emotion is transient. However, there are features of how we value and choose that are always present, persistently directing the way we judge prospective outcomes. For we assess not in absolute terms, but *relative to what we have* - we favor results that give us more. Known as "reference dependence," this was pointed out by psychologist Daniel Kahneman and is part of the reason he received the 2002 Nobel Prize for Economics.[148] Unfortunately, in the long term, 'more' is often harmful.

An event from my farming past shows this. When I was young, there were a hundred acres or so of natural forest on an adjoining farm. It was a valuable, renewable reserve – it gave timber, nests for pest-eating birds, and shelter for stock. Then it was cut back to form a clump along the top of a hill, with the 'freed' land put into growing wheat. After I went to secondary school, it was cut again. It stayed undisturbed for another twenty years, and then was reduced once more - and now all the timber was gone.

Over fifty years, three generations of farmers had cared for that little forest, each generation generally taking less than half. Until ultimately, they had removed all of it.

55

Why? It was not because the farmers were poor – each family made a more than adequate living. It was because each cut of the forest meant a little more income from wheat, and each generation could not resist the temptation of having 'a little more.' All those 'little more's finally added up to 'all'; the pleasurable small gains of wheat demolished the whole forest.

The attractiveness of 'more now' is a massive challenge for humanity and our finite planet. It means our wants can never be met; they are limitless. 'More' is never 'enough.'

As well as wanting more, we avoid 'having less.' If a loss threatens, we gamble to prevent it, even if this risks a more significant loss - this is called "loss aversion."[149] An associated bias is that we enjoy rewards that come soon, even if they diminish or reverse in the future. Together, these biases mean we take more than we need. If our living planet is to have a future, we have to cease our greed and decide for the long-term.

But we also like events that end well

Happily, there is a preference that opposes the attractions of 'more' and not less. For the way we feel about an event also depends on how it ends.

In an iconic experiment, Redelmeier and Kahneman investigated the amount of discomfort reported by patients during and after colonoscopy. They found no relationship between the duration of the procedure, or the total amount of pain reported, and the patients' later evaluation of the experience. Instead, the patients' assessment was predicted by the most intense pain reported during the procedure and the average amount of pain reported over the last three minutes.[150] It has become known as 'the Peak/End rule.'

This finding supports the common expression 'alls well that ends well' and is evident across a wide range of experiences. For example, people give significantly lower ratings to environmental conditions that worsen over time, compared to events that remained the same or improve.[151] It applies to lives too - a life that ends abruptly at a good point is judged better than one with more mildly pleasant years, known as the 'James Dean Effect.'[152]

We all prefer situations that change for the better or end in a good position compared to those which become worse. Moreover improving conditions offer a healthier future than deteriorating ones. To save our environment, this preference is one we must encourage.

Reimagining the situation

While we use time travel to make choices, the results are not just dependent on accurate scenarios and how we judge them, for we can change these same scenarios and outcomes by manipulating our beliefs. For material changes are not necessary for greater happiness – altered expectations and hopes can achieve this without them.

An imagined state can bring happiness and success

This is shown in our appreciation of music, and the Stradivarius violin in particular. The Stradivarii are sublime violins: they stand head and shoulders above contemporary instruments. We are told this, and we believe it, and love to hear them, as do experts in music.

However, *their superiority is not technically true* – we actually can't tell the difference. When three esteemed experts listened to three vintage violins and a modern one, no expert identified more than two of the four violins, and two of the experts identified the contemporary violin as the Stradivarius.[153] In a later test, twenty-one experienced violinists played vintage violins and high-quality new instruments under blind conditions. The most-preferred violin was again a new one, the least preferred was a Stradivari, and most players were unable to tell whether their most-preferred instrument was old or new.[154]

Blind tests have failed to find a superior sound for the Stradivarius - experts don't know a Stradivarius from a modern quality instrument.

What this means, is that it is our *belief*, not the sound, that generates the extraordinary listening pleasure that devotees of the Stradivarius report. One would expect the same with pop music - if you are a Jimi Hendrix fan, once you think the song is Hendrix, you love it. Nor do beliefs only change our experiences in music. They also alter our sense of taste - the more costly you believe a bottle of wine to be, the more pleasurable is its flavor.[155]

As well as enhancing our pleasures, beliefs reduce pain. When Benedetti and co-workers gave patients drugs for pain and anxiety, those who knew of the treatment reported more relief than those who did not; we know this as the placebo effect. Similarly, drawing attention to treatment makes it more productive - a sham acupuncture needle gives more relief than a placebo pill.[156] And there is a converse effect - negative expectations cause more suffering, the "nocebo effect."[157] About sixty percent of patients undergoing chemotherapy start to feel sick before the treatment.

Favorable anticipations also ward off illness. An optimistic temperament in nuns and university graduates was found to mean good health in later life[158], and religious belief to reduce the depression caused by adverse life events, the anxiety of difficult tasks, and the likelihood of death.[159] Positive expectations strengthen our physical and our mental health. Nor does faith have to be real. I did not believe in God as a teenager, but a short prayer still allowed me to sleep soundly before exams. I weaned myself off the habit as I grew older. It seemed hypocritical.

Belief gives career success too. Self-belief predicts performance in university, sport, and everyday life.[160] It allows a scientist to champion a break-through idea, and a tight-rope walker to advance across a chasm. "No pessimist ever discovered the secrets of the stars, or sailed to an uncharted land, or opened a new heaven to the human spirit," said Helen Keller.[161] Life-affirming beliefs don't have to be correct to support us; we only have to believe them.

And when belief takes the form of hope, it is a lifesaver. The ancients recognized this; Pandora released all the evils from her jar into the world, yet hope remained. Amnesty International Australia asked refugees what was most valuable to them. They answered, "hope for a better life." Halina Birenbaum's memoir of life in Nazi death camps revealed the same. Halina said she did not want to believe in death, and "preferred any lie a hundred times, as long as it gave me hope of surviving." Her book was called "Hope is the last to die."[162]

After all, we spend most of our time waiting for the future to come, so we want to expect good events. Marx was only partly right. It is hope, not religion, that is the opium of the people. The power of belief reveals a new path - a good future does not have to be real, we just have to believe in it.

Forming rose-colored futures, or 'cooking the books'

Not only is a fictional happy-future as good as a real one, it is also easier to form - we can just *invent* a good future.

And we do. Our ability to originate desirable futures allowed my mother to say, "nothing is either good or bad, but thinking makes it so." I never understood this homily - it seemed to mean 'good' did not exist. But my mother, and Shakespeare, were right.[163] For we use story-telling to create what we would *like* to happen.

We form a story that explains how our future will be happy, or why our current, unfortunate state, may already be so. If our circumstances are dire, we re-interpret them, and thus endure. As pointed out by George Orwell, "we are all capable of believing things we know to be untrue."[164]

Indeed all the plans we build for ourselves may be part lies - a mix of cause and effect sequences telling us what to do, plus a sprinkle of fictionalizing to keep our emotions smooth[165].

Sometimes this embroidery concerns the form of the events, and at other times their importance. When I was a consultant, I often had two projects running, for example, developing a quality of life measure, and another identifying demand for hospital services. If one had difficulties, I would say to myself, "everything is ok - the other project is fine, *and it's more important*!" My morale then improved, and I could work well on both. Without such self-intervention, I would have become depressed and functioned poorly.

We routinely re-write history to make our circumstances palatable; we adjust even when confronted with minor concerns. If a friend cancels an after-work drink, I may initially feel down, but then I remind myself of another upcoming event, and I feel fine. And it's not only me; whole communities can change their attitude when there is no choice. In 2007, an expanded US military base in Italy was announced and met with general opposition, but the population then formed beliefs to support it, and the reception changed to positive. [166]

Telling ourselves soothing stories is an essential part of us. It is recognized in the talking therapies that are a mainstay of mental health services. Here we are coached to reinterpret events, change beliefs, and form a positive way forward. Hence in 'rational-emotive behavioral therapy' uplifting and motivating thoughts are substituted for negative ones – 'I failed at this relationship, so I am a failure,' becomes, 'I have learned from this, and next time I will know better.' We fortify ourselves with tales that allow us to go on.

Talking therapies work well; they improve depression and anxiety, and can be more enduring than medication.[167] Internet-based psychotherapy is also useful, as well as positive motivational books.[168] And we can do it by ourselves – just writing about traumatic events helps.

This raises the question of how do we create these stories. There is an easy answer to that - we apply the same mental kit that we use to explain the physical world. After all, the narratives we use to explain the material world and ourselves only *could* be real. Often, they are not. And, as mentioned earlier, we use similar processes when we 'confabulate.' That is when we explain those of our behaviors that we don't understand.

As to whether story-telling *originated* to explain the material world, our-self, or to form reasons for happiness, we don't know. But it is at least conceivable that story-telling arose to give us hope, and with it the energy to go on, and only later did we form stories to explain ourselves and the physical world.

Living in the present and ignoring the future

Believing in a happy future is not our only aid to overcoming challenges. If future events are disastrous and imminent, we *suppress* the unfavorable - we concentrate on the immediate present and don't think about the future.

This was described in the book *A Woman in Berlin*, a memoir of April 1945. The anonymous author, along with other women in Berlin, was awaiting the occupying Russian army - they were expecting the city to be sacked and the women to be raped. How did they cope? The author said they focused on the scarcity of sausages, they "fled into the present to escape worrying about the future." Later, when under bombardment, the women again avoided fear by focusing on small emergencies, like damage to the water pipes. The author said that when living in the present, "you don't think - you don't even feel afraid, because you're so distracted and absorbed."[169]

A similar reaction was described by Halina Birenbaum when a young girl in the Majdanek death camp. She said she concentrated only on staying alive, and in this way, reduced her awareness of cruelty and suffering.[170]

We do this with other crises too. The single-handed ocean sailor Frank Mulville said that when conditions are life-threatening, "preoccupation with the immediate problem, however threatening the conditions, will insulate [the lone sailor] and envelop him in a psychological cocoon."[171]

Doing both

Often both devices will be operating – we suppress worrying thoughts while maintaining positive ones. This seems to happen with the severely-ill. Adang and others found in 1998 that cancer patients avoided saying they felt worse unless they experienced a substantial down-turn, but they would report feeling better after only *a little* improvement. Other studies have found similar. Kidney transplant patients waited until they felt better before describing their pre-transplant state as 'bad,' and patients with severe postoperative pain did not report it until they had improved.[172] These patients ignored outcomes that disagreed with what they preferred to be happening.

Another example is maintaining a preferred view as an inevitable event approaches, and then changing it when the event is about to occur, what has been called the 'hot/cold' difference.[173] For example, women may decide on natural childbirth without analgesia, but change their minds once the time comes. Or we may declare we will never enter a nursing home, but as we get old, decide we have to.

Sometimes we change too late. We adopt a desirable fantasy because of the pleasure it brings, only to be shocked back into reality by taking it too far. I remember this illustrated in a Peanuts cartoon: Charlie Brown wrote a letter telling a girl how much he liked her, smiling as he took the message to the postbox. But when he posted it, he was aghast! In place of 'she loves me,' he thought of all that could go wrong, and now it could not be changed.

One might assume that suppression and fictional story-telling is operating in some that deny climate change. If reality is miserable, some may focus on a pleasant fiction to keep being happy as long as they can.

We can switch as feelings dictate

Sometimes we choose an account from which we soon have to back-peddle. I found this when having relationship problems. My thoughts went like this.

- Just before a break-up: *"I am thinking only of reasons why we should be apart... and how to break up"*. I was concentrating on thoughts opposing the relationship, although a part of me was aware I might later change my mind.
- Having broken-up: *"I am feeling desolate and alone, and anxiously constructing reasons to be together."* Now I was suppressing the "should be apart" reasons, although deep down, I was vaguely aware that if we did get back together, they might again emerge.
- After a partial rapprochement: *"I am concerned about a repetition of the bad experiences."* Now the "should be apart" reasons re-appeared.
- Finally, later but still unresolved: *"I am trying to put all the issues on the table, but I can't."* I was struggling to be as honest as I could, but the information from the various 'glasses' conflicted and would not co-exist in my mind.

In brief, the experiences and arguments that I was aware of depended on my bias at the time. While I did not *intentionally* ignore opposing reasons, my feelings seemed to drive and corral my reason-finding so only a sub-set of factors jostled at the front. The rest were functionally invisible, as though a wall blocked out part of my mind.

Why in switching my positions did I suppress awareness of the downsides? What benefit was there in not seeing possible adverse consequences, given it took away my chance to avoid them?

One possible explanation is that when no path is paramount, the best strategy is to target the one with the most desired outcome and try to make it work (while free to switch again later, if we fail). And for that, we must suppress opposing arguments. This is what seems to happen in confirmation bias, as discussed earlier - we make a choice and then blind ourselves to information that opposes it. In that case, I suggested we do so to allow us to act (avoiding indecision). Perhaps something similar applies here; seeing all sides may not always help, sometimes it is better to choose what offers the most desired outcome and go for it (it will give us temporary happiness, at least).

Happiness maps

Through story-making, suppression, and time-traveling, we develop plans and select futures. The result is a *'happiness map.'* This map, or narrative, gives us an account of events and reasons for hope. It 'puts things into perspective,' allowing us to 'live in the best of all possible worlds,' our natural state, according to the fictional philosopher Dr. Pangloss (in *Candide*, Voltaire's parody of philosophical optimism). It also tells us how we can realize a desirable future. The neurologist Oliver Sacks observed we all create narratives; he said they are:

> ... *constructed, continually, unconsciously, by, through, and in us — through our perceptions, our feelings, our thoughts, our actions, and, not least, our discourse, our spoken narrations.*[174]

Yet life is not static. As we follow our map, our plans are re-written by real life. Jobs are lost, relationships fail, we experience illness and injury, and our nation goes to war. "No plan survives contact," stated Von Moltke, the great Prussian military tactician.[175] So we rebuild. We reconsider our situation, look at events and circumstances afresh, amend our predictions, and our plans, seeking to survive both emotionally and physically. We do so until we arrive at a new set of strategies and expectations, one that again offers a desirable future. We have re-formed the future in our imagination and created a template to achieve it in real life. We carry out this rebuilding continually.

From life coach to life destruction

So we change our happiness maps. We do so not only because events change, but because we are trying to achieve what can be incompatible objectives – a stress-free life in the present, and desired outcomes in the future – and there is no one right way to accomplish this. In fact, we have available a range of potential map-plans, and I will illustrate four. Two offer a future without damage to ourselves or others, and two are harmful.

The first is '*The life coach.*' Here the map achieves a beneficial and harm-free balance based on realism. We are doing well in our studies, so we form a plan to go to graduate school - we will 'study hard' and have a great future. This map adopts a realistic view of our situation and forms practical answers. It may even allow mechanisms that conflict with our experience but are none the less accurate (as science does with the bizarre world of quantum mechanics).

This plan is a practical way forward, but it does ignore a little of what could go wrong to ensure we are not too stressed. In an egalitarian, peaceful, affluent community, a plan offering both happiness and a secure material future can be realistic. People who have it available are very fortunate.

The second is '*The survivor.*' Now our program contains much fantasizing. It is mostly an optimistic dream, but some awful situations require it. If our circumstances are terrible, an unvarnished narrative of causes and effects is not appropriate - brass-tacks realism could produce panicked fight, flight, or immobilizing depression. In such a case, a pie in the sky is better. Our feelings are critical to our ability to carry on, and finding a dream/goal that will bring us happiness in the present is all we can do.

Such is needed when survival is threatened, as is the case with persecuted refugees in a war zone, or patients dying of a terminal disease. Facing death, we have a last defense: we tell ourselves half-truths, and shift our focus to achieving an *inner* equilibrium. We formulate our suffering as salvation and our misery as martyrdom. This type of map helps us subsist emotionally, even in a concentration camp. Now delusions /dreams are not a mistake, for they help us and do no harm to anyone else. In a situation where the future is bleak, we shield our feeling-self.

Peaceful, free, affluent societies have less need for these happiness-making dreams. Still, even there (and I live in such a place), people can require to keep their spirits up - our children may have an incurable illness, or our partner is leaving us. By weaving an optimistic future, we can ward-off fear, and keep from paralyzing worry. This map can be an excellent source of support. In some awful states, it is a godsend.

Now the third type of plan, '*The self-harmer.*' Here the genie of self-delusion is well and truly out of the bottle - we gain happiness by forming stories that allow us to damage ourselves. Our desires cry, 'bring me happiness,' and we suppress any thoughts that hinder us from gratifying our wants, substituting reasons that allow them. Drug-taking becomes 'living on the edge,' and unsafe sex practices 'a low likelihood risk.' We abuse our ability to re-write circumstances, and form beliefs that offer short-term pleasure in exchange for self-injury. Our ideas now give us damaging outcomes. We self-inflict harm, and we fail to see it.

But there is a worse form of happiness map. The fourth, '*The life-destroyer.*' Here we harm others, usually for personal benefit. In the most severe case, we kill, as when white people invaded and occupied Australia in the 18th and 19th Centuries. Australia's white colonists murdered the indigenous peoples to occupy their lands, the killing documented in 19th Century colonial records which refer to "settlers up the country dropping the natives as coolly as if they were speaking of dropping cows." Their justification was that Aborigines "are not human, or hardly... killing them is no murder."[176]

Nazism in the 20th Century is another example. In both cases, a physically stronger group took the possessions of another, and killed them. In both, the slaughter was justified by saying the victims were sub-human.

In forming the 'life-destroyer' happiness map, story-telling receives its ultimate challenge and abuse. I remember hearing an interview with a Khmer-Rouge leader. He said intellectuals are the best soldiers. A peasant might say, "Why should I kill this old man - he has not hurt anyone," but a revolutionary intellectual will declare, "In the name of the revolution, I will kill all of them."

In the 1946 New York Times interview with Einstein, the one mentioned at the beginning where he appealed for a change in how we think, he went on to say, "it is easier to denature plutonium than to denature the evil heart of man."[177] His gloom is understandable. Our ability to justify harm cannot be over-stated.

White-collar life destruction

There is a variant of 'life-destroyer' where the harm-doing is less apparent, more hidden away, but still damaging. This is mainstream or 'white-collar' destruction, where modern democratic governments adopt policies and practices that harm. I have been a party to it. In the 1980s, I was involved in the restructure of psychiatric services in an Australia state. The policy was backed by an ideology that said psychiatric institutions were undesirable, while community based-services were beneficial. This doctrine allowed funding authorities to close mental hospitals and make substantial cost savings, even though the community support services to replace them did not as yet exist.

Such actions require acceptance by the electing population, but this, unfortunately, may be gained without too much difficulty. Kind people may overlook even obvious harm if subjected to the blandishments of self-interest, and given an excuse for doing so. This is illustrated by ordinary hypocrisy - we accumulate possessions while lamenting environmental destruction, or disable animals in the laboratory while caring for pets at home; we gain by harming and contradict our values.

Once we have accepted an excuse for doing harm, even worse can happen - a multiplier effect. Each time we choose to believe a falsehood or condone a harmful action, we are less able to see the harm we do. Our lies reconceive how we see our situation, changing the sentiments we attach to events. Once formed, these fictional beliefs remain in our minds to muddy our perceptions, poison our reasoning, and misdirect our thinking.

And here's the rub. Self-interested delusion is probably the greatest threat to ourselves and the natural world. Its possessors will accept demolition of a forest with little or no empathy for its animal inhabitants, and ignore the repercussions that harm us all. Yet all the while, they know they harm, offering fabrications as excuses, such as 'our immediate needs must be met.' For our ongoing pillaging of nature is usually accompanied by such deceits, allowing habitats to be obliterated, rainforests cleared for oil palm, and the inhabitants displaced and killed, including indigenous peoples and our cousin primates (e.g., orang-utans). These convenient beliefs allow us to kill other creatures and damage the planet, destroying natural habitats, and those who live there. Those who merely 'pass-by' are equally guilty, for whether they commission, execute, or tolerate habitat-clearing and animal deaths, they are supporting the 'life-destruction' of our world.

Why we destroy so readily

We can now reconsider a question I raised at the beginning. Why do we destroy so readily? We have the answer – it is because invention and destruction are two sides of the same coin.

As we have learned, we employ imaginative story-telling to understand the physical world. However, we also use it to create fictional futures. With story-telling, we can see what we like and ignore what we don't - data from real events is not needed to allow our preferred course, 'evidence' from imaginative fictions will do the job. If our feelings crack the whip, we can justify anything, including harming for personal gain. Telling ourselves stories gives us opportunities without limit - if we are a leader, it will let us launch war, or environmental Armageddon.

Not that justifying with fictions is always wrong - the majority of the stories we form will cause little or no harm. Indeed some are of great benefit - if created to give hope in a concentration camp, self-delusion can be a savior, and a false account of circumstances lets people with incurable cancer rate their quality of life as 'good.' Some dreams may even bring glory: we can achieve the seemingly impossible if we think we can; our capacity to re-conceive circumstances can be a beautiful thing.

However, when we form falsehoods to justify harm, we commit our most prominent thinking 'mistake.'

Summary: assess long-term, and no lies

In the domain of the self, we seek to answer questions like 'do I want this,' and 'will it make me happy.' We aim to achieve what pleases us. To do this, we assess courses of action based on the feelings aroused in 'time-travel,' where we imagine potential futures and mentally inhabit them.

Time-traveling is a fascinating means of assessing options and making choices, but there are dangers. We act impulsively and make choices we later regret. We also take more than we need and down-play the future (while we may judge wisely for a year ahead, we don't consider fifty years; 'more now' is not a recipe for long term survival). And we falsify scenarios - while story-telling is a beautiful gift that lets us understand and cope, it also means we can overlook threats or justify harm for personal gain.

We must change. In big decisions, we need to assess futures comprehensively, consider long term outcomes, and eliminate self-deceit.

So how well do we decide in the realm of our inner-self? High competence will exist in some individuals; they will avoid the numerous pitfalls and assess carefully. But for most of us, there is work to be done. Despite our efforts in psychology, business, and psychiatry, we deserve a modest score. I suggest five out of ten.

For a good future, we must all become '*thorough time-travelers.*'

A thorough time-traveler -

- Identifies and values *all* the possible consequences of a proposal, including those they prefer not to exist
- Decides when calm, and not when feeling emotional
- Requires that long term outcomes are positive – they are deciding for their grandchildren
- Rejects courses justified by fictions
- Does not lie to themself (unless it only does good)

CHAPTER 4.

A Brave Rabbit
Shows Us What
Is Right

Parts of the picture developed in this project have been worrying, in particular, how we justify whatever we find pleasurable, such as a short-term gain, even if it harms others.

Fortunately, there is a further domain of thinking, one contained *within us* - our sense of right and wrong. Formed by feelings, upbringing, and beliefs, our moral sense tests the proposals before us, and in doing so, makes us better people.

The value of values

Secular or religious, and in a double act with feelings, ethical principles guide what we do. Some concern only our individual selves, while others, which I will call public ethics, are promoted by whole societies.

Public ethics promote desirable behaviors and prohibit harmful ones. In written form, they are relatively recent – we homo sapiens have been around for about three hundred thousand years, but it is only in the last five thousand or so that belief systems have been recorded. Often they reflect religious proclamations, although religious traditions would go back far earlier (perhaps they were an evolutionary development to stop us from destroying).

Moral principles (or ethics, or principles of right and wrong) tell us how to act. From about 600 BC, Zoroastrianism taught of the need to struggle for good - "Ohrmuzd" against the evil "Ahriman," while Buddhism taught us to control desire. Then, from 300BC to 500AD, Stoicism, the ethical system of educated Greeks and Romans, emphasized how we should manage ourselves, to control feelings such as greed. Christianity and Islam have advocated related values.

These principles have been regularly refined to produce safer and more just societies. In the 19th and 20th centuries, western countries legislated against slavery, developed rules for warfare, and in some places, curtailed capital punishment. In the 21st Century, there have been changes liberalizing marriage and sexual relationships, and permitting euthanasia. The record has not been perfect, but we have changed the guidelines for our behavior to make life safer and more just - we have revised our ideas of what is right and wrong, and upgraded our beliefs.

We need world-protecting ethics

Now our principles need further reform, as we face substantial external threats.

The most recent is the coronavirus pandemic, which, while dangerous, is none the less controllable. The others are of our making, and much more severe. One is the prospect of nuclear war. It has been with us for more than seventy years; we created it, and it has never gone away. Another is population expansion, but humans are now experiencing decreasing fertility, and the number of people is forecast to decline after 2064 (from a maximum of 9.73 billion, compared to7.8 billion in 2020).[178]

The third and last is the dual challenge of environmental degradation and climate change. This is a huge threat, one we must fight.

We have been taking as we wish from the natural world, and the consequences are severe. Our international representatives are anxious. In May 2019, Sir Robert Watson, Chair of the United Nations IPBES Global Assessment body, said: "The health of ecosystems on which we and all other species depend is deteriorating more rapidly than ever. We are eroding the very foundations of our economies, livelihoods, food security, health, and quality of life worldwide." The UN committee concluded that the widespread destruction of natural ecosystems now threatened the extinction of 1,000,000 species.[179]

Global warming has led to similar warnings, and calls for action. On 23rd September 2019, the UN Secretary-General António Guterres closed a Climate Action Summit with the words, "We need more concrete plans, more ambition from more countries and more businesses. We need all financial institutions, public and private, to choose, once and for all, the green economy."[180]

The changes to our natural world are severe. Humanity faces dying seas, broken ecosystems, and climate chaos. These events are not unexpected or the result of some malign external force - our damaged environment reflects the actions of humans over hundreds of years. The consequences of our activities have long been apparent; scientists have been sounding alarm bells for decades. But we have been unwilling to see the danger or change our behavior, and a small number have continued to champion land clearing and resource exploitation. Some of us have become concerned and agitated for change, but most have looked away.

Why have people continued these destructive practices? Some may gain, in the short term. Others will be under pressure from denying colleagues or wish to conform, lemming-like, to the views of their leaders. A few individuals will not want to contradict their earlier statements or admit they were wrong. And the remainder might be explained by self-delusion or distrust of science.

Whatever the reasons, we must stop making excuses, and move to protect our natural environment. The time has come (it is overdue) to put nature on an equal footing with humans; we have to restore nature's balance. We possess the principle 'don't harm people,' but we need one to stop the harming of our living world. We require a new moral value of 'cherish and protect nature.'

How to install a new value?

How do we get people to adopt a new value of protecting nature? We can make laws requiring us to care for the living world. Some nations already have them. The Constitution of Ecuador now has a Chapter "Rights for Nature," which states that nature in all its life forms has the right to exist, persist, maintain, and regenerate. An ecosystem can be named as a defendant equally with humans,[181] and people have the legal authority to enforce these rights on its behalf. And in New Zealand, a river (known by the Māori as Te Awa Tupua) has been given the legal status of a human to protect it – guardians can represent it in a court of law.[182]

On the other hand, passing such laws requires popular support, and currently, many people and nations will reject protecting wild nature - they may not make such laws, or if formed, enforce them (what they take from the natural world is too pleasurable).

How can we be sure of getting humans to adopt new ethics, ones that in the short term may have a personal cost? A sense of intellectual approval is not enough - we often fail to do what we should; we routinely have 'qualms' but ignore them (manufacturing reasons to do so). However, as we now know, feelings guide decisions, and if we learn to place a high emotional value on nature, we may succeed in firing-up protective laws.

There are two ways to develop such feelings – by heightening awareness of the consequences of environmental collapse, and by strengthening people's concern for the welfare of our planet's wild creatures and plants.

Fear of environmental destruction

To take the first approach, most know the environment is deteriorating, and this is harmful to all - media have long reported the dangers. People are aware that a world without balance is an unstable place, that the loss of living nature would endanger us, and its degeneration harms us. Because of this, many have an underlying sense of foreboding.

For we rarely succeed in totally suppressing worries. Feelings tend to go undercover, present but denied. This has been shown with illness. Vanderzee et al. in 1996 found that people with cancer *reported* life satisfaction equal to healthy persons, but data revealed higher rates of clinical depression.[183] And Epstein et al. in 1989 found that family and friends rated chronically ill patients to have lower emotional health than the sufferers themselves, suggesting they saw signs the patients were trying to deny.[184]

The same applies when the challenges are solely emotional – we may find reasons to argue everything is ok, but we are not convinced. I remember my girlfriend proposing we live apart. I struggled to find a silver lining, and eventually lit upon, "I will be financially better off and can pursue my hobby of sailing." I could almost believe it, and it kept my emotions stable - but I was still unhappy. We don't even escape our worries through sleep. Lewis Carroll observed, "Again and again I have said to myself, on lying down at night, after a day embittered by some vexatious matter, "I will not think of it anymore!" ... and in another ten minutes I have found myself, once more, in the very thick of the miserable business, and torturing myself."[185]

Why don't we build stories that eliminate our worries? There are various reasons. Some of us are poor at emotion regulation, perhaps through traumatizing experiences. Others are nagged by regret (for example, breast cancer patients suffer more distress if they feel they have received sub-optimal treatment).[186] But the most likely reason, is the need to survive - ignoring the issue might hurt or even kill us. If an illness remains uncured, or if we stay unemployed, or we don't stop smoking, we have to do something about it.

So, until our problems are solved, they will remain in our minds to pester us. Unless global warming and destruction of nature stop, we will continue to feel apprehension - there will be an undercurrent of disquiet, and a desire to protect ourselves.

We can use this awareness to create restorative values.

Placing our self in another's shoes

The second way to promote a protect-nature ethic is to build on our concern for the world's wild creatures. Many already feel deeply about the world's extraordinary diversity of animals and plants, and want to protect them. These feelings are a form of empathy, and we know this is powerful. "Simply by putting oneself into the shoes of another ... one may instantly feel pain, sympathy, or other vicarious emotional responses," said Haidt.[187] We feel empathy with animals from childhood. A toddler will wonder at a snail and want to care for it,[188] and a little boy will look up at his daddy while patting a puppy and say, "I think he likes me."

Caring for animals and plants - and sometimes geographic features too - was once central to being human. Many First Nations peoples still feel a responsibility for the natural world - the indigenous peoples of Australia have held such views for sixty thousand years. And recent destructive events have aroused empathy in all of us, as we witness the struggles of marine animals mired in plastic, the clearing of Amazonian jungles, and the advance of terrifying Australian bushfires.

We can support these feelings. We can boost empathy by pointing out the ways of other living things. We can show that animals are 'people' too.

For they are.

Animals are people

Let me explain. I grew up on a 'wheat and sheep' farm on the Wimmera plains of Victoria Australia. When I was about sixteen, my father told me there were several wild rabbits behind the large shed where we kept our heavy farm machinery. It was my job to control their numbers. I took the single-shot .22 rifle and went there just before dusk.

Slowly, the rabbits appeared. Soon there were five - two parents and three young. From about thirty yards, I shot the doe. She tumbled over and over and over from the impact of the bullet, then lay without moving. I reloaded and shot one of the kittens; it jumped high in the air, fell straight down, and lay still. Now all that was left was a buck and two young, about twenty-five yards away, all seemingly frozen in shock. The father was smaller than a domestic cat and much less intimidating.

Then, totally unexpectedly, the buck charged. He ran straight at me, until at only four yards away he stopped, lurching from side to side, barking hoarsely as if asthmatic, trembling so violently he could barely stand. He looked up into my face. He seemed terrified, but he stood his ground and faced me. I remained still. I watched him.

Then I let the butt of my rifle fall to the ground, turned, and walked home. I left him and his two remaining young. His charge was the bravest act I have ever seen. I have never shot another rabbit.

Animals empathize with each other

Rabbits are not the only animals that care for their kinfolk. On the farm, I would walk the cold paddocks in the lambing season with my father, reuniting lost lambs with their mothers. I saw the agitation of both and their joy at finding each other.

There are many reports of animals caring for their own. The literature describes, for example, a magpie grieving over its dead partner, the protection of herd members by elephants, distress in a goose when it's mate fights with another, and concern showed by lizards, llamas, bear-cubs and bonobos.[189]

We have also observed the empathy of animals in laboratory experiments. Displaying our human heartlessness and dubious morality, we have found that mice react more to pain if they watch cage mates' in similar distress, and are more anxious if they see suffering in mice who they know. They also show more discomfort from stomach pain if they are with other mice when all are fed irritants.[190] And we have observed compassion, at a cost to the helper: a free rat will release a cage-mate if it is trapped, and let it share its food[191], and rhesus monkeys will *not* pull a chain to deliver foodstuff if it means another will receive an electric shock.[192]

On the other hand, predator animals are mostly indifferent to the feelings of their prey - seeing the eyes picked out of a living lamb by farm-crows taught me that. And in this, they are the same as humans. When I was young, graziers would routinely hang a sheep upside down then cut its throat. With the occasional exception; my father would shoot it first, the only farmer I knew to do so.

Animals read other's minds

Animals also understand what their own kind are thinking - non-human primates may realize the intents of others other in a way similar to a four-year-old child.[193] Birds, too, understand intentions, and they deceive. Scrub-Jays hide their food stores from other Jays and relocate them if seen. And if a potential thief is about, they hide food in quiet soil trays, not noisy pebble ones. Revealingly, Jays only exhibit this behavior if they have stolen from other Jays; if they take, they expect others will.[194] In other words, they read minds as humans do.

Animals mind-read *other species* too. Working Border-Collies stop sheep breaking from a mob, dissuading each imminent escape move with a slight motion of the canine head or paw, anticipating and preventing break-aways one after another, with dexterity greater than a soccer goalie. And they "mentally time travel," for they plan much as we do. If sheep escape from the mob, the dog will 'feint' to mislead them, then circle back behind and round them up.

Sheepdogs also learn the ways of humans. When working, they are careful not to hurt the sheep - nipping at heels is ok, no more - otherwise, there will be trouble. If they do maim or kill a sheep, it is typically under cover of darkness, and then they stay away from their farmer-owners, displaying a wariness and anxiety that keeps them absent for days (and for a good reason, for on returning they are shot dead). Dogs 'mirror' our feelings too, in "sympathetic yawning," and know to look at the right side of human faces to see if we are happy or angry.

Dog mind-reading is also shown in games. A human and a dog will play together with a ball, the canine engaging in the game (enthusiastically, as does the human), anticipating the next throw, each happily retrieving. Both have little doubt about the game being played and their part in it. Humans anthropomorphize to understand dogs, and they 'canomorphize' to understand us.

On this basis, attributing motives could be an efficient way for humans to understand many animals, although scientists have traditionally opposed thinking of animals in this way.

Animals solve problems

Animals are problem-solvers. Over eighty years ago, Wolfgang Kohler demonstrated that chimpanzees could solve mechanical problems. He suspended a banana above and out of reach, and observed a chimp move a box to below the banana, and then spring up and grab it.[195] More recently, we have found that New Caledonian crows create hooks by cutting a stepped pattern into the edge of leaves, and use these to remove insects from plants.[196]

And there is much evidence of other cognitive similarities. Animals exhibit cerebral laterality (for example, the octopus),[197] understand numbers,[198] and engage in rapid-eye-movement sleep (which, in people, is related to dreaming).[199] They have personalities too; within one species, some sharks are loners while others are social. And they have senses we lack - a dog's sense of smell is a thousand times more sensitive than humans,[200] fish detect electric pulses, and the mantis shrimp can see from the ultraviolet to the infrared as well as polarised light.[201] Animals are aware of things that we are not.

To sum up, people and animals are alike. Some animals are very similar: they show stress and anxiety, give mutual care, empathize, problem-solve, and mind-read. Many animals may think like us; images and feelings seem central to human thinking, and there seems no reason why higher animals should not also think using mental pictures and emotions. In this respect, Darwin considered thinking didn't need language. He felt the thought of animals would be like ours, differing only in degree.

By and large, animals and people are made of the same stuff – genetically, physically, behaviorally, and emotionally. One could even argue that some animals are morally superior. Humans justify harming with verbal reasoning - we can talk our empathy away. But as animals lack words, they presumably cannot engage in this trickery, which may explain why many people find emotional closeness with a pet so very special - dogs could be more 'humane' than we are.

In conclusion, animals both need and deserve our empathy. And we know from personal experiences we are capable of it. When we see a wild tortoise crossing our path, care for a pet at home, donate to care for animals harmed by bushfires, or offer water to backyard birds, we sense how they feel.

A stopping function

If we can grant other living creatures our compassion, we will wish to extend them our protection. Some of us already do; in India, Jain priests sweep the path before them as they walk, so as not to kill a single ant.

Through the power of empathy, our care will be armed with a visceral sense of right and wrong, powerful and felt right now, rooted in deep emotion, an ethic based on strong personal feelings. Protecting the natural world as part of ourselves will become part of our conscience, and we will have a belief that can save us - for by feeling empathy for our living world, we will have a 'stopping function.'

In robotics, if a soccer-playing robotic 'dog' is about to run into a wall, it will be stopped in its tracks - this is the specific job of one particular sensor. Other sensors try to win the game; this one only stops the robot from destroying itself. In our context, a feeling and belief that nature is our family, and we must protect and care for it, can barricade proposals that would destroy our natural world. We will have an emotion-charged counter-weight to forestall looking away when harm is done, and we will stop accepting long-term damage for short-term benefit. At the least, we will have a clear guide to good behavior.

The result will be *two* forces to underwrite a new set of values - fear of what might happen if nature's systems collapse, and the need to love and protect our world's wild creatures. With the two, we can create a code of caring for all living things, placing as much importance on wild animals and plants as we do humans.

Summary: protect our living world

Ethics inform our actions. The way we decide in the domain of right and wrong is guided by moral principles, particularly those bolstered by strong feelings. These principles fortify us to make the right decisions and help us avoid the wrong ones.

However, to do their job, to do what is right and not what is wrong, our ethics have to be up to date - and currently, they are not. Once our greatest danger was atomic war, and 'mutually assured destruction' (MAD) was why we must avoid it. Now we have another MAD - if we kill nature, then we will die too. We have a MAD via environmental catastrophe.

All that keeps us from potential devastation is a rapidly diminishing natural world. Countless species share our planet and our DNA - fish, whales, frogs, trees, birds, possums, meerkats, elephants, pets, primates, and penguins - and our survival is linked to theirs. Yet public values to protect our environment are mostly absent – our feelings, consciences, and ethics permit the destruction of the world's wildlife and their habitats. We have to upgrade our values; we require an invigorated conscience and a nature-protecting ethic.

All of us have to protect nature. Those who currently oppose such protection need to realize the danger of such thinking, and undergo a change of mind.

Fortunately, we humans can transform our views. It has happened before. The great Indian military leader Asoka was an example - he whose sign, the wheel, forms the center of the Indian flag. In the third century BCE, Asoka unified almost all of India through violent conquest, then realized the damage he had done, saw the horror of war, and became a Buddhist. For the remaining forty years of his reign he required compassion to be shown to all creatures, man and beast.[202]

Some consider Asoka to be the greatest monarch who ever lived. The precedent he has set is big enough for even the most hardened climate change denier, or champion of forest clearing.

And there is a cautionary reminder from an even earlier age. Around 2400 BC, the Egyptians thought the human heart revealed one's character. They believed that, after death, each person's heart is weighed against the feather of the goddess Maat, standing for what is true and right. If the heart weighed more than the feather, the bearer was lost (s/he was consumed by a monster).[203] Unfortunately, the heart of humankind seems heavy; currently, we lack Maat's values of balance, harmony, morality, and justice. We have to upgrade our moral principles if we are to save ourselves.

Our performance in the domain of knowing right from wrong appears to be perilously inadequate. I won't hazard a guess as to its score. However, many recognize the vital importance of caring for the natural world and examine their hearts regularly - seeking to do what is right and not what is wrong. I will call such people *'informed sages.'*

An informed sage -

- Develops clear values and follows them
- Is well-informed, and ready to upgrade their understanding of what is right and wrong
- Cultivates empathy with all living things
- Adopts and vigorously promotes the value 'cherish and protect nature'

We all need to become 'informed sages.'

CHAPTER 5.

All The Truth And Half The World

The temple of Apollo at Delphi contained the inscription, "Know thyself."[204] In this book, I have done my best to follow that advice. In doing so, I have discovered the wonder of our thinking - we explain and decide in four thinking worlds, unique domains of thought that lie nested within each other, our four Russian dolls.

Unfortunately, our current way of thinking is a danger to us and our living world. Others have expressed concern, not only Einstein. For example, the novelist Ian McEwen was accompanying an arctic survey when he became annoyed at the team's failure to cooperate in storing boots. It was a trivial matter, but he was forced to conclude, "We will not rescue the Earth from our depredations until we understand ourselves a little more."[205] And the naturalist David Attenborough ended a report on overpopulation and environmental destruction with the appeal, "Can our intelligence save us?"[206]

However, the most prescient was Colin Wilson in his 1967 allegorical novel *The Mind Parasites*, where he warned of failings in human thinking. In the book, alien beings had invaded the *minds* of people, hindering deliberation, and sapping creativity. Yet people did not realize, they felt their thoughts were acceptable and normal, they had to overthrow the parasites before they could reason clearly.[207] We seem to be in the same position as Wilson's people - we display shortcomings in each of our thinking worlds.

Our quandary may require us to visit all four domains of thinking, but only one mistake is needed to make the decision a poor one. Take, for example, the chopping down of a forest. Our thinking in the domain of the *Material World* may urge caution – the broader consequences of forest clearing will be unknown. The *People* domain may also advise care - many people inherently dislike change to our natural world. On the other hand, if the forest's demise means personal gain, the *Self* domain will favor it strongly, based on short-term self-interest. "In the race of life, always back self-interest, at least you know it's trying"; that is how the Australian Prime Minister Paul Keating would have put it.[208] And as for the fourth domain, that of *Right and Wrong?* If we have no values that argue one way or the other, it will acquiesce. The result? We will clear the trees, and hang the consequences (and justify our actions with story-telling).

But why are our unwise tendencies so hard to see, or at least to stop? Maybe, as I suggested earlier, they once worked well, and we adopted them as part of us. "Those things most important to us are hidden by their simplicity and familiarity," said the philosopher Ludwig Wittgenstein.[209] Einstein, too, felt we have wrong beliefs embedded in us – he suggested false axioms about mass, space, and time lie within us, and this is why Special Relativity Theory was so hard to comprehend.[210]

Whatever their origin, it is time our thinking mistakes came to an end. We must recognize our faults and correct our thinking errors.

All the truth

We know the changes needed so we can see the truth. We now have to implement them.[211] Details are given in the earlier chapters, but I will briefly review them.

A questioning world thinker in the physical world

In the material world, we have to become 'world thinkers.' Humankind has learned a great deal about the physical world; we have shown genius here. Now, as individuals, we require to understand science and apply it in our lives. We need to examine events, encourage diverse ideas, and change our understanding in line with the evidence.

As it is, we too often seize to wrong ideas and treat unwillingness to change one's mind as a virtue. When Margaret Thatcher said: "This lady is not for turning," we praised her. Similarly, we criticize a politician's change of position as a "flip-flop." Instead, when there is new evidence or a more precise understanding, we have to adopt it.

An inquiring mind reader in the world of people

We have to become smarter in how we relate to people. To interact with others, we rely on spontaneous empathy, a beautiful and valuable capacity, but a dangerous one. Reflex judgments of people, automatic mind-reading, can lead us to trust a charlatan, or discriminate merely because the other person is different. We have to learn about people to understand them, and form an 'Applied Science of Humans' to help us. We need to assess people intentionally and openly declare our views (independently of seniors, groups, and leaders).

We also have to increase the role of females in all decision-making. We require their openness, cooperation, and ability to solve problems.

A thorough time-traveler in our inner self

When making personal decisions, we choose what makes us happy. Mental time-traveling is an ingenious method, but an unreliable one. To decide well, we must identify all short and long term outcomes (including those we don't like), and assess them calmly.

We also must value results for the long-term, and stop spinning arguments that let us harm others or the planet.

An informed sage in the world of values

The fourth is the most crucial realm. Here we halt ruthless proposals and promote those we believe in.

Unfortunately, our values are out-dated. 'Human interests come first' (so woodchip the wild forests) means long term harm to all. To stop our living planet imploding, we require a new one: 'Cherish and Protect Nature.' We have to adopt this ethic, encourage it, and apply the principle passionately and fearlessly. Our survival may require it.

A moratorium on half the world

When making big decisions, the sources of error in the four thinking worlds must remain before our eyes - now, we will know the flaws and how to correct them. But that is not enough. Time is slipping away, and the big problems - those of wilderness destruction and environmental chaos - won't wait. Thinking better will help, but that will take time to be adopted, and our poor thinking has already done far too much damage. Our living planet is dying; the number of people has more than doubled in the last forty years,[212] but the number of wild animals has halved.[213] As well as thinking wisely, we need to act in immediate, practical ways.

Science panels

First, we must have information to help us; we need scientific reports as inputs to our reasoning. However, scientific papers may become compromised (zealots can ridicule them as questionable or biased), and partisan politics might discredit concerns. We need reviews of evidence, and action recommendations, that cannot be sidelined.

I suggest establishing national science panels to provide impartial scientific information. The committees would provide annual or biannual reports without the influence of party politics. Their advice would be free and accessible to both the parliament and the public. How to determine the issues to be addressed would need to be determined, but should include referrals from the government, parliament, and the panels themselves.

Separate assemblies would cover the physical, biological, behavioral, and social sciences (at least), with composite or further groups created as required. All panel members would require advanced expertise suitable to their panel specialty, and be allocated limited terms (subject to approval by, say, a two-thirds majority of parliament).

The government would not be obliged to respond to these reports, but the people would judge the government's response (or lack of it) at the ballot box.

Protecting and restoring habitats

As well as public access to independent scientific information, we need comprehensive habitat protection. An example is Raine Island, the largest rookery in the world for the green turtle. Located in the Australian Great Barrier Reef, Raine Island is a protected area for turtles and sea birds.

Each year 60,000 green turtles migrate thousands of kilometers to lay their eggs there. When they leave the reef as tiny hatchlings, it takes a further thirty years before they reach maturity and return to lay their eggs. I once heard a biologist say, "what they find on their return will depend on what humans have chosen to value and protect in the meantime." The island is under threat, and the turtle population is in decline. To save these little turtles, we must support their cause; they do not have the language to argue their case. The same applies to many other species.

Forming or enhancing wilderness reserves will not be straightforward - we need steps that now seem fanciful. An idea put forward by the biologist E.O. Wilson is that half the surface of the Earth be left to function as it was before modern man.[214] He recommended this include the California redwood forests, the Amazon River basin, and the grasslands of the Serengeti, estimating this would conserve about eighty percent of existing species.

Other scientists have made similar suggestions. The Global Deal for Nature, too, proposes that fifty percent of our planet be kept in a natural state.[215] If we return large areas of land and sea to the natural world, we can halt the juggernaut of humans. We can start to reverse the damage done, to re-balance humanity and the environment.

The survival of wilderness is more important than economic benefits to humans. There are already plenty of alienated lands for towns, agriculture, and manufacturing. And there can be unpredictable consequences when one shrinks ecosystems or reduces their diversity; a healthy natural world aids our survival too.

Protecting fifty percent of the earth as wilderness is an appropriate and proper aim - it indicates that we value nature and humans equally.[216] We can let Mother Nature develop beauty and intricacy in its myriad of forms. And at the same time, we humans, on our half of the world (or halves, as each nation would provide its fifty-percent share), will create, engineer, and enjoy *our* version of beauty.

Then, if a future celestial traveler should call by, and ask how we created such a beautiful planet, we will be able to answer, "with all the truth and half the world."

A New Type
Of Thinking

Science, arguably our greatest social accomplishment, gives us a structured account of the universe, a way to investigate, and a process for determining our situation and options. We can overcome almost any problem with this extraordinary method. Yet, things have not gone smoothly. We have failed to care for nature. We harm the natural world, and ourselves.

The reason is not technical. It is not because, say, we are unable to understand how ecosystems work, or what drives the climate. Our great weakness is not our inability to understand the physical world. It is to do with old impulses and processes that have been unchanged for millennia - the way we decide what to do.

Let us return to Evariste Galois. Even though he faced imminent death, he ignored the threat and worked on his mathematics. Why? Perhaps it was due to the status he gave mathematics; maybe he considered it more important than his life. But more likely, it offered him an escape from worry (in the way that the women of Berlin avoided fear by focusing on a shortage of sausages). If Evariste had not pursued his mathematical distractions, he might have confronted the threat of the duel, and taken steps to call it off. Furthermore, while we don't know the details, perhaps the fight was agreed to in the heat of the moment, and had he waited till he was calm, he may have found another way.

Two hundred years later, we face environmental chaos and the loss of countless living beings that legitimately inhabit our earth, creatures that have done nothing to deserve elimination. Again, the reason is weaknesses in our thinking, although probably a different cluster to that which caused Evariste's death. For we have ceded our living world in exchange for short-term gains, aided by artful, self-defeating story-telling. We have refused to see the truth.

Equality between earth's creatures

To save ourselves and the natural world, we have to change. We have to tear up our devil's pact and alter the way we reason and decide – and adopt a new moral value.

Gus Speth, former Dean of the Yale School of Forestry and Environmental Studies, realized the critical role of emotion-rich values in environmental matters. He said:

> I used to think that the top environmental problems were biodiversity loss, ecosystem collapse, and climate change [and science could address them]. However, "the top

> *environmental problems are selfishness, greed, and apathy*
> *... we need a cultural and spiritual transformation.[217]*

My investigations have led me to the same conclusion as Gus Speth. I had thought we might solve our problems with clear thinking, but I found that to redirect our way of living, we must change our moral principles. Only through a value upgrade can we be sure of protecting our living planet.

Currently, we are homocentric. Our view of nature considers only human needs, and largely excludes wild plants and animals; our values are focused on protecting people. To protect the *whole* of the living world, we must enlarge our vision. For damage to the remaining wilderness is accelerating, with unforeseeable consequences, and a principle of general equality of living creatures is required. We must add the moral value, 'Cherish and protect nature.'

Of course, that is not all. We need changes to the other thinking domains too, the mental worlds of material things, people, and our inner self. Only when all are corrected can we be truly free of our 'parasites.'

Can we upgrade our values and reasoning and restore our natural world? We can, but it will not be easy. Nietzsche said, "It is not courage of our convictions that we need, but courage for an attack upon our convictions."[218] That maxim applies here - to overthrow the old ways, including stopping the pillaging of nature, we need a revolution, and for this, our resolution must be robust. Many social and political obstacles will have to be overcome, and we must be steadfast and brave and prosecute our new guiding beliefs - pallid lip-service is not enough.

We can do it. Humans have made big changes before – Buddhism, Stoicism, Christianity, and Islam, are examples - and this can happen too. We can transform how we see ourselves and other living creatures to become nature's friend and ally, not its enemy.

And that stance will save us. For in accepting that nature has equal rights to humans, the destruction of our natural world becomes indefensible. We will tackle our mental errors, and we will remediate our planet. We will change how we reason to create a better, safer world.

We will have a new type of thinking.

Appendices

A checklist for making decisions is in Appendix 1; important meetings might have this printed on attendee notepads. Possible ways to improve ourselves are in Appendix 2.

Appendix 1. A checklist for decisions

This list is for those pondering a significant decision. Circle 'Yes' if you are doing as recommended, 'No' if you are not. A 'No' suggests the issue needs further examination.

1. Concerning the material world

a. *Follow the approach of science.* Observe, imagine, and test, forming views based on evidence, not prestige or authority. Yes or No.

b. *Check perceptions.* Clarify what you see, don't be blinded by what you expect, fear, or desire. Yes or No.

c. *Consider alternative explanations and courses of action.* Look out for a better idea. The right decision may need it. Yes or No.

d. *Change your mind when the evidence says to.* Yes or No.

2. Involving people

a. *Deliberately explore what others think and feel.* Don't assume you know; automatic sensing is often wrong. Yes or No.

b. *Don't defer to others, particularly to leaders or groups.* It is in the interest of all that we judge independently and speak our minds. Yes or No.

3. Gaining happiness

a. *Identify all the outcomes.* Including those that argue against your preferred course. Yes or No.

b. *Do nothing when transported by emotion.* Strong feelings change how we assess even neutral events. Wait until calm, and reconsider before acting. Yes or No.

c. *Don't favor short term gains or gamble when it could mean a worse outcome.* 'More now' is seductive and never satisfied, and may lead to undesirable consequences. Yes or No.

d. *Be suspicious of any fictional reasoning.* We lie to ourselves if it brings us happiness or gain. Self-delusions are only acceptable if they help and do no harm. Yes or No.

4. Testing with our sense of right and wrong

a. *Ensure your values are up to date and well informed.* Yes or No.

b. *Reject propositions that violate your principles.* Yes or No.

c. *Empathize with all living things.* Yes or No.

d. *Protect nature equally with people.* Yes or No.

Appendix 2. Ways to improve ourselves

We all engage in faulty thinking, including this book's author (as my anecdotes have shown). I offer the following suggestions to help improve our views and ideas.

The World

❖ List five or six beliefs you hold, which you know other people may reject. Then, for each view, write two specific reasons why your opinion could be wrong. Next, return to your list and see if you wish to revise your stance, identifying any you are now unsure of. Lastly, apply any new open-mindedness in a productive way, such as discussing your revised views with others.

People

❖ Ask your friends, family, or acquaintances, including at least one from a different culture, about their ideas in an area such as politics, religion, or global warming. Merely inquire, don't judge. Note where their views are different from what you expected.

❖ Identify an issue where you think there is a better way of doing things, an idea you believe could be of benefit to all. Then raise it with your boss, colleagues, or clients. Without being overbearing, make your case sincerely and confidently.

Your Inner Self

❖ Think of an occasion when you have acted too hastily through feeling strongly, and resolve that next time you will wait until you are calm.

❖ Identify a significant course of action that you are considering, work, or personal. Then investigate and list all its desired outcomes in both the short and long term. Next, investigate and list all the possible *undesirable* outcomes, again both short and long. Lastly, consider whether you still favor it.

❖ Consider where you are harming others by favoring your personal interests. Cease doing so, or at least reduce the harm you are doing.

Right and wrong

❖ Identify your values, and where needed, revise, and update them.

❖ Recognize where you are violating your values, or suppressing or ignoring them. Find ways to behave that are not in conflict with your principles.

❖ Stop harming the natural world. No more excuses, just stop. Then begin a new drive to care for plants and animals sustainably.

❖ Join actions, or act alone, to call out prominent figures who persist in nature-harming practices.

❖ Donate time or money to protecting wildlife/wild nature, at least equal to what you do to help people.

❖ Grow plants that may offer food to native birds and animals.

❖ Reduce consumption of non-degradable or energy-intensive materials. Avoid single-use materials or packaging. Have a sit-down coffee, not a non-degradable cup; get a 'keep-cup.' Practice re-cycling as best you can, then challenge yourself to do better.

❖ Reduce your use of water, heating gas, transport fuel, electricity - showers from eight to four minutes (saving ten gallons for the environment each time, plus the energy used to heat it). Save petrol; take a bus instead of driving. Save electricity, turn off lights.

❖ As a voter, examine your choices to ensure those placed in power protect the natural world.

❖ Talk with friends and family and see what they do. Show your protective and sustainable ways.

Thank You!

Bibliography
Notes

[1] On Galois: Rothman T. 'Genius and Biographers: The Fictionalization of Evariste Galois.' American Mathematical Monthly, 89, 84 (1982).

[2] Quote: Einstein. "Many persons have inquired concerning a recent message of mine that 'a new type of thinking is essential if mankind is to survive and move to higher levels.' Often in evolutionary processes a species must adapt to new conditions in order to survive. Today the atomic bomb has altered profoundly the nature of the world as we knew it, and the human race consequently finds itself in a new habitat to which it must adapt its thinking." .... "It is easier to denature plutonium than to denature the evil heart of man." From 'The real problem is in the hearts of men,' an interview with Michael Amrinc published in the Sunday Magazine section of the New York Times on 23 June 1946, as reported in 'Einstein on Politics: His Private Thoughts and Public Stands on Nationalism, Zionism, War, Peace, and the Bomb,' Edited David E. Rowe & Robert Schulmann, Princeton University Press, 2007. Einstein maintained this concern, and just days before his death in 1955, he signed the Russell–Einstein Manifesto, calling for international conflicts to be resolved peacefully.

[3] Carr EH. 'What is History?' Penguin Books. 1961, p. 23

[4] Quote: "define a cause to be an object followed by another, and where all the objects, similar to the first, are followed by objects similar to the second." Hume D. 'An Enquiry Concerning Human Understanding' 1748

5 Helen Keller: 'Helen Keller, The Story of My Life.' Houghton Mifflin Co., 1905

6 Quote: "if we fancy some strong emotion." James W. 'What is an Emotion?' in Essays in Psychology (Cambridge: Harvard University Press, 1983), 173–4

7 Recognition-primed decision making: Klein G. 'Sources of power. How people make decisions.' The MIT Press, Cambridge Massachusetts, London England 1999

8 Quote: "I see only one move ahead." Ross, P.E. 'The Expert Mind.' Scientific American, Aug 2006, Vol. 295, Issue 2

9 In their mind's eye: Klein G, Klinger D. (1991). 'Naturalistic decision making.' Human systems IAC gateway,2(1), 16 – 19; Zsambok CE, Beach L, Klein G. A literature review of analytical and naturalistic decision making. Task 2. Final Technical Report. Prepared by Klein Associates Inc, for Naval Command, Control and Ocean Surveillance CenterResearch, Development, Test, and Evaluation Division. Submitted: 31 December 1992.

10 Quote: 'Clearly in one's head.' Liljedahl P. 'Mathematical discovery: Hadamard Resurrected.' Proceedings of the 28th Conference of the International Group for the Psychology of Mathematics Education, 2004 Vol 3 pp 249–256

11 Quote "I left Caen." Lecture given by Henri Poincare to the Societe de Psychologie in Paris, reported by Jacques Hadamard in 'The Psychology of Invention in the Mathematical Field,' Dover/ Princeton University Press, 1954, p.12.

12 Quote: "When you are taking a shower." Muller B. 'The Creative Landscapes Column: Creatovation.' AI & Soc (1998) 12:296-303;

[13] Quote: "I had nothing to do." Feynman RP. 'Surely You're Joking, Mr. Feynman!' New York: W. W. Norton, 1985 pp. 157–158.

[14] Quote: "Imagination is more important than knowledge." The Saturday Evening Post, 'What Life Means to Einstein: An Interview by George Sylvester Viereck', 1929 October 26.

[15] Quote: "We don't need any more experiments." Cooper LN. 'On the problem of consciousness.' Neural Networks 20 (2007) 1057–1058

[16] We think in images about a quarter of the time: Heavey CL, Hurlburt RT. 'The phenomena of inner experience.' Consciousness and Cognition, Volume 17, Issue 3, September 2008, Pages 798-810.

[17] Understanding how devices work: Rozenblit & Keil 2002, cited by Keil FC. 'Explanation and understanding.' Annu. Rev. Psychol. 2006. 57:227–54

[18] Kekule's snake: Rothenburg A. 'Creative cognitive processes in Kekule's discovery of the structure of the benzene molecule.' American Journal of Psychology 108.n3 (Fall 1995): pp419(20)

[19] Holes through the points of spears: Krippner S. (1981). 'Access to hidden reserves of the unconscious through dreams in creative problem-solving.' Journal of Creative Behaviour, 15, 11–22.

[20] Wegener saw continents moving like icebergs: Solomon M. 'Scientific Rationality and Human Reasoning'. Philosophy of Science, Vol. 59, No. 3 (Sep. 1992), pp. 439-455.

[21] Einstein thought in more or less clear images: Hadamard J. 'The Psychology of Invention in the Mathematical Field,' Dover/ Princeton University Press, 1954, p. 142

22 Feynman diagrams: Miller A I. 'Cosmic Imagery'. The Times Higher Education Supplement – 21 August 2008.

23 Picasso's cubist ideas: Miller A.' Second Sight: Les Demoiselles d'Avignon'. New Scientist. 26 September 2007

24 Einstein's thoughts were also muscular: Hadamard J. 'The Psychology of Invention in the Mathematical Field,' Dover/ Princeton University Press, 1954, p. 142. Also see Bohm D and Peat FD. 'Science, order, and creativity.' Routledge Classics. 2000

25 Feynman whoops: Root-Bernstein RS. 'Music, Creativity, and Scientific Thinking.' Leonardo, Vol. 34, No. 1, pp. 63–68, 2001

26 It may have been on the ABC (Australian Broadcasting Commision) Radio National 'Science show', but that's all I can remember.

27 Search model versus the logogen model: O'Connor RE, Forster KI. 'Criterion bias and search sequence bias in word recognition.' Memory & Cognition 1981, 9 (1), 78-92

28 Thomas Kuhn: Bird A. 'Thomas Kuhn,' The Stanford Encyclopedia of Philosophy (Spring 2013 Edition), Edward N. Zalta (ed.)

29 Feyerabend 'old ideas contaminate facts': Godfrey-Smith P. 'Theory and Reality: an introduction to the philosophy of science.' The University of Chicago Press Ltd, Chicago and London, 2003. P.111-116.

30 Karl Popper held that scientists have to think outside prevailing notions: Godfrey-Smith P. 'Theory and Reality: an introduction to the philosophy of science.' The University of Chicago Press Ltd, Chicago and London, 2003. P.107.

31 The EU means different things: Deutsche Vella interview with Norbert Mappes-Niediek. 'Europe is the powder keg - the Balkans are the fuse,' 17.02.2017

[32] Quote: Feynman 'how can it be like that.' Aharonov Y, Rohrlich D. 'Quantum Paradoxes - Quantum Theory for the Perplexed.' 2005 Wiley-VCH Verlag GmbH & Co. KGaA, Weinheim. ISBN 3-527-4039 1-42005.

[33] Equations were the one part all can understand: See Bohm D, Peat FD. 'Science, order, and creativity.' Routledge Classics. 2000; Rees M. 'Mathematics: The only true universal language'. New Scientist. 11 February 2009

[34] Paul Dirac: Rees M. 'Mathematics: The only true universal language'. New Scientist. 11 February 2009

[35] BACON: Klahr D, Simon HA. 'Studies of Scientific Discovery: Complementary Approaches and Convergent Findings.' Psychological Bulletin, 1999, Vol. 125, No. 5, 524-543; Bohm D, Peat FD. 'Science, Order and Creativity,' Routledge, 2nd ed. 2000

[36] Very interesting mistakes: Goro Shimura said of Japanese mathematician Yutaka Taniyama (1927 –1958) that 'he was not a very careful person as a mathematician. He made a lot of mistakes. But he made mistakes in a good direction. I tried to imitate him. But I've realized that it's very difficult to make good mistakes.' Fermat's Last Theorem. BBC Horizon. 1995.

[37] Quote: "A more primitive mode of thought." Wilson EO. 'The diversity of life,' in Dawkins R. 'The Oxford Book of Modern Science Writing.' Oxford University Press, 2008, p. 145.

[38] Quote: "stopped thinking in concrete visual images.' Barrow JD. 'Cosmic Imagery: Key Images in the History of Science,' The Bodley Head, 2008, cited by Miller AI in his review of Cosmic Imagery. The Times Higher Education Supplement – 21 August 2008

[39] Quote: 'whether it appears in the robust form.' Gribbin J. Erwin 'Schrodinger and the quantum revolution'. Black Swan. 2012. P. 53, 54.

[40] Quote 'the primates who tell stories.' See Dawes RM. 'A message from psychologists to economists: mere predictability doesn't matter like it should (without a good story appended to it)'. Journal of Economic Behavior & Organization. Volume 39, Issue 1, May 1999

[41] Experience-honed intuition: Hadamard J. 'The Psychology of Invention in the Mathematical Field', Dover/ Princeton University Press, 1954

[42] Diagnostic experts: Groves M, O'Rourke P, & Alexander H. 'The clinical reasoning characteristics of diagnostic experts.' Medical Teacher, 25, 308-313.

[43] Foreign country: Maddux W, Adam H, and Galinsky AD. 'When in Rome ... Learn Why the Romans Do What They Do: How Multicultural Learning Experiences Facilitate Creativity.' Personality and Social Psychology Bulletin 2010 36(6) 731–741.

[44] Vedantam S, Schmidt J, Shah P, Boyle T. 'Creativity And Diversity: How Exposure To Different People Affects Our Thinking'. NPR July 27, 2020. See https://www.npr.org/2020/07/27/895858974/creativity-and-diversity-how-exposure-to-different-people-affects-our-thinking?

[45] Answers while dozing: Fechner's Law. Robinson G H. 'Fechner's Law.' Corsini Encyclopedia of Psychology. 2010

[46] At awakening: Hadamard J. 'The Psychology of Invention in the Mathematical Field,' Dover/ Princeton University Press, 1954; p. 8.

[47] Dreams: Stone MD. 'Creativity in dreams.' In M. A. Carskadon (Ed.), Encyclopedia of sleep and dreaming (pp. 149-151). New York: Macmillan. 1993

[48] Mathematical problems: Hadamard J. 'The Psychology of Invention in the Mathematical Field,' Dover/ Princeton University Press, 1954; p. 8.

[49] Making sense of odd connections: Angry Penguins. http://australia.gov.au/about-australia/australian-story/angry-penguins

[50] See: Hadamard J. 'The Psychology of Invention in the Mathematical Field,' Dover/ Princeton University Press, 1954

[51] Walt Disney: Muller B. 'The Creative Landscapes' Column: Creatovation. AI & Soc (1998) 12:296-303

[52] Luck: Klahr D, Simon HA. 'Studies of Scientific Discovery: Complementary Approaches and Convergent Findings.' Psychological Bulletin 1999, Vol. 125, No. 5, 524-543

[53] Chance and trial & error: Klahr D, Simon HA. 'Studies of Scientific Discovery: Complementary Approaches and Convergent Findings.' Psychological Bulletin 1999, Vol. 125, No. 5, pp 524-543

[54] Clever naturally: TT Genotype. S Keri. 'Genes for Psychosis and Creativity' Psychological Science, 2009, Volume 20, Number 9, 1070-73; Einstein and spatial reasoning. Balzac F. 'Exploring the brain's role in creativity'. Neuropsychiatry reviews, Vol 7, No. 5, May 2006.

[55] Intelligence: Heilman KM, Nadeau SE, Beversdorf DO. 'Creative Innovation: Possible Brain Mechanisms.' Neurocase, Volume 9, Issue 5 October 2003 , pp 369 – 379; see also Gabora L. 'Cognitive mechanisms underlying the creative process.' In T. Hewett and T. Kavanagh, Eds. Proceedings of the Fourth International Conference on

Creativity and Cognition, October 13-16, Loughborough University, UK, 2002, pp. 126-133.

56 Monitoring by our unconscious is revealed when we suddenly hear our name loud and clear at a cocktail party, while other words are lost in noise: Moray N. 'Attention in dichotic listening: Affective cues and the influence of instructions.' Quarterly Journal of Experimental Psychology 11 (1): 56–60. 1959.

57 Quote: "If you are not afraid now and then." In: Sarah Motherwell, Ben Spraggon, Nathan Hoad, and Tim Leslie. 'Twelve boys, a football coach and 10 kilometers of caves. What could go wrong?' Australian Broadcasting Commission News. 13 Jul 2018.

58 Feynman on 'gleaming': Miller. 'A thing of beauty" 50 NewScientist, 4 February 2006

59 My thesis: O'Connor RE, Forster KI. 'Criterion bias and search sequence bias in word recognition.' Memory & Cognition 1981, 9 (1), 78-92

60 Einstein noted: Hadamard J, 'The Psychology of Invention in the Mathematical Field', Dover/ Princeton University Press, 1954, p. 142

61 G.B.Dantzig: lbers and Read 1986, cited by Movshovitz-Hadar N, 'Intellectual courage and mathematical creativity,' Proceedings of The 5th International Conference on Creativity in Mathematics and the Education of Gifted Students. Haifa, Israel, February 24-28, 2008.

62 Wegener on icebergs: Solomon M. 'Scientific Rationality and Human Reasoning.' Philosophy of Science, Vol. 59, No. 3 (Sep. 1992), pp. 439-455. Solomon also noted that Wegener's example had been cited as supporting disagreement in scientific communities, that conflict leads to

concentrated activity and debate until the issue is settled and maybe a scientific advance

[63] On developing ideas alone: Liljedahl P. 'Mathematical discovery1: Hadamard resurrected.' Proceedings of the 28th Conference of the International Group for the Psychology of Mathematics Education, 2004 Vol 3 pp 249–256.

[64] More likely to cry at movies: Seider BH, Shiota MN, Whalen P et al. 'Greater sadness reactivity in late-life.' Soc Cogn Affect Neurosci 2010

[65] A study of US college students: Heavey CL, Hurlburt RT. 'The phenomena of inner experience.' Consciousness and Cognition, Volume 17, Issue 3, September 2008, Pages 798-810.

[66] Limitations in attention - person in gorilla costume: Simons DJ, Chabris CF. 'Gorillas in our midst: sustained inattentional blindness for dynamic events.' Perception, 1999, volume 28, pages 1059-

[67] Shanteau: Shanteau J. 'Psychological characteristics and strategies of expert decision makers.' Acta Psychologica 68 (1988) 203-215; Kahneman, D. & Klein, G. (2009) 'Conditions for intuitive expertise: A failure to disagree.' American Psychologist 64:515–26

[68] Limitations in memory, US Space Shuttle Challenger: Neisser & Harsh 1992, cited Phelps EA. 'Emotion and cognition: Insights from Studies of the Human Amygdala.' Annual Rev. Psychology. 2006. 57:27–53

[69] Confused when receiving bad news: Maltzman JD. 'An Ironic Ordeal of an Accomplished Oncologist' The true story of Dr. Vincent Caggiono and his wife Biba, a professional chef and breast cancer survivor. OncoLink, Abramson Cancer Center of the University of Pennsylvania. Posting Date: June 26, 2005.

[70] 'Switching faces'. Hall L, Johansson P. 'Choice blindness: You don't know what you want.' New Scientist, 15 April 2009,

[71] Forming false memories: Johansson P, Hall L, Sikström S, Olsson A. 'Failure to Detect Mismatches Between Intention and Outcome in a Simple Decision Task.' Science 7 October 2005: Vol. 310. no. 5745, pp. 116 – 119; Disneyland. Braun, Ellis, & LoRus, 2002, cited Loftus, E.F, Bernstein D M. (2005). 'Rich False Memories: The Royal Road to Success.' In A. F. Healy (Ed) 'Experimental Cognitive Psychology and its Application'. Washington DC: American Psychological Association Press, p 101-113.

[72] Primed by irrelevant cues - crime as virus versus beast: Thibodeau PH, Boroditsky L. 'Metaphors We Think With: The Role of Metaphor in Reasoning.' PLoS ONE 1 February 2011 Volume 6 Issue 2 e16782; we can also view our own future adversely, if we have recently been alerted to bad events. Västfjäll, Peters and Slovic 2007, cited Böhm G, Brun W. 'Intuition and affect in risk perception and decision making.' Judgment and Decision Making, Vol. 3, No. 1, January 2007, pp. 1–4

[73] Video-fight. Hagemann N, Strauss B, and Leißing J. 'When the Referee Sees Red ...' Psychological Science August 2008 19: 769-771

[74] Quintillian: Frost M. 'Greco-Roman Analysis of Metaphorical Reasoning,' 81 J. Legal Writing Inst. 113, 115 , 1996.

[75] Attractive woman. Bertrand M, Karlan D, Mullainathan S et al. 'What's Psychology Worth? A Field Experiment in the Consumer Credit Market.' Economic Growth Center, Yale Univesity, Center Discussion Paper No. 918, July 2005; see also Critcher CR and Gilovich T. 'Incidental Environmental

Anchors.' J. Behav. Dec. Making (2007); Englich B, Mussweiler T, Strack F. 'Playing Dice With Criminal Sentences: The Influence of Irrelevant Anchors on Experts' Judicial Decision Making.' Personality and Social Psychology Bulletin, Vol. 32, No. 2, 188-200 (2006);

[76] Primes can be dangerous: Cigarette packs silver and gold. Hammond D, Dockrell M, Arnott D et al. 'Cigarette pack design and perceptions of risk among UK adults and youth.' The European Journal of Public Health, September 2, 2009.

[77] Confirmation bias: Nickerson R. 'Confirmation Bias: A Ubiquitous Phenomenon in Many Guises.' Review of General Psychology, 1998, Vol. 2, No. 2, 175-220. Other terms are focalism, ascertainment bias, faulty triggering, rapid narrowing, and set effect. For example the "focusing illusion" was defined as the human tendency to make judgments based on attention to only a subset of available information, to overweight that information, and to underweight unattended information - Schkade and Kahneman (1998), cited Chugh D, Bazerman MH. 'Bounded Awareness: What You Fail to See Can Hurt You.' Harvard University 10/15/2004. Downloaded on 23 May 2013 from http://www.people.hbs.edu/mbazerman/Papers/Bounded%20Awareness.pdf A form of focalism is also evident in groups, which typically adopt the most commonly held opinion instead of seeking the best.

[78] Signs of both muscular and musculo-skeletal disease: Kostopoulou O, Mousoulis C, Delaney B. 'Information search and information distortion in the diagnosis of an ambiguous presentation.' Judgment and Decision Making, Vol. 4, No. 5, August 2009, pp. 408–418

[79] Quote: of William James on carving out order. James W. 'A Pluralistic Universe.' Hibbert Lectures at Manchester

College on the Present Situation in Philosophy. 1909. 'For another [man], again, there is no really inherent order, but it is we who project order into the world by selecting objects and tracing relations so as to gratify our intellectual interests. We carve out order by leaving the disorderly parts out; and the world is conceived thus after the analogy of a forest or a block of marble from which parks or statues may be produced by eliminating irrelevant trees or chips of stone'.

80 Logogen versus search models: O'Connor RE, Forster KI. 'Criterion bias and search sequence bias in word recognition.' Memory & Cognition 1981, 9 (1), 78-92

81 Wilson's disease: Groopman J. 'How Doctor's Think.' Mariner Books. 2008. P.46, 47.

82 Diagnosis momentum: Groopman J. 'How Doctor's Think.' Mariner Books. 2008 P. 128; Marc J. Shapiro, Pat Croskerry, and Steven Fisher. 'Profiles in Patient Safety. Sidedness Error.' Academic Emergency Medicine Volume 9, Number 4 326-329

83 Divorce judges: Shafir E. 'Intuitions about rationality and cognition.' In 'Rationality: Psychological and Philosophical Perspectives,' ed. KI Manktelow, DE Over, pp. 260–83. Florence, KY: 1993

84 Hindsight bias: Fischhoff B. 'Hindsight [not equal] Foresight: The effect of outcome knowledge on judgment under uncertainty.' Journal ol Experimental Psychology: Human Perception and Performance, 1975, Vol. 1, No. 3, 288-299 (Reprinted in Fischhoff B. 'Hindsight [not equal] foresight: the effect of outcome knowledge on judgment under uncertainty.' Qual Saf Health Care 2003;12:304–312); See also Fischhoff B. 'For those condemned to study the past: heuristics and biases in hindsight.' In: Kahneman D, Slovic P,

Tversky A, eds. Judgments under uncertainty: heuristics and biases. Cambridge: Cambridge University Press, 1982: 335–51; hindsight bias may also explain the over-confidence we can have in our understanding of mechanisms - people may rate their understanding of how a helicopter or a zipper works as 'high', only to revise their view when asked for details. 'The illusion of explanatory depth.' Keil FC. Explanation and understanding. Annu. Rev. Psychol. 2006. 57:227–54

[85] Hindisght bias: Arkes HR, Wortmann RL, Saville PD, and Harkness AR. 'Hindsight bias among physicians weighing the likelihood of diagnoses.' Journal of Applied Psychology. Volume 66, Issue 2, April 1981, Pages 252-254

[86] Quote: of Stephen Jay Gould on ascent of man. Summary Review of a talk given at McGill University on November 4, 1998, sponsored by the Redpath Museum and the Department of Biology.

http://astro1.panet.utoledo.edu/~ljc/Gould_pat.html (downloaded 30 May 2009)

[87] 'Studied calm' is advisable: Groopman J, 'How Doctor's Think'. Mariner Books. 2008. Quotes Harrison Alter; p. 74.

[88] Eliminating bias: Arkes HR, Faust D, Guilmette TJ, et al. 'Eliminating the Hindsight Bias.' Journal of Applied Psychology, Volume 73, Issue 2, May 1988, Pages 305-307

[89] Quote: of British Royal Society in its 'Directions for Seamen Bound for Far Voyages', in Preston D & M, 'A pirate of exquisite mind: The life of William Dampier', Corgi Books, 2005. P.18-20.

[90] Sir Isaac Newton: F=GM1 x M2/r2. Godfrey-Smith P. 'Theory and Reality: an introduction to the philosophy of science.' The University of Chicago Press Ltd, Chicago and London, 2003 P. 93. Note some areas of research investigate

causes before effects, such as seeking neural-mechanisms underlying emotions in the absence of an adequate description of how emotions are expressed (perhaps reflecting the advent of fMRI). Note also that narrative explanations, made up of strings of cause and effect relationships, need repeated confirmations under differing circumstances by different experimenters before one can accept them.

91 Hypothetico-deductive method (also termed 'falsificationism'): See 'The Logic of scientific Discovery' published by Popper in German in 1935 and in English in 1959. To apply Popper's approach one deduces a hypothesis from a theory, and then attempts to show it is false. Because of this, Popper said that Marx's and Freud's theories were not scientific, as no matter what happens a Marxist or a Freudian can fit it into his theory.

92 There is no authority, even Newton was found wrong: Godfrey-Smith P. 'Theory and Reality: an introduction to the philosophy of science.' The University of Chicago Press Ltd, Chicago and London, 2003. P. 58, 59, 60.

93 Parsimony: this maxim has been criticised as practically useful but hard to justify - see Godfrey-Smith P. 'Theory and Reality: an introduction to the philosophy of science.' The University of Chicago Press Ltd, Chicago and London, 2003 P.214. One also needs to be ever aware that any cause and effect relationship may be limited to specific circumstances. For example in pharmaceutical drug trials patients are often highly selected in terms of age range and presence of other illnesses (so as to minimize variability and assist detection of any effect of the drug), but the result may be that the effects found (if any) apply only to patients with those particular characteristics.

[94] Worms in the science apple: Martinson BC, Anderson MS, de Vries R. 'Scientists behaving badly.' Nature. Vol 435, 9 June 2005: failing to present data contradicting one's own research (6%), excluding data based on a 'gut feeling' that it was wrong (15%), or changed the design, methodology or results of a study in response to pressure from a funding source (15%).

[95] The origins of the phrase seem unclear: for example, see https://en.wikipedia.org/wiki/He_Ain%27t_Heavy,_He%27s_My_Brother

[96] Amnesty International: News letter from Amnesty International Australia, 19 Feb 2015, from actioncentre@amnesty.org.au

[97] Halina Birenbaum 'the touch of his hand': P.178, in Birenbaum H. 'Hope is the last to die: A coming of age under nazi terror.' M. E. Sharpe, Armonk New York, 1996

[98] Emotion contagion: Wild B, Erb M, Bartels M. 'Are emotions contagious? Evoked emotions while viewing emotionally expressive faces: quality, quantity, time course and gender differences.' Psychiatry Research. Volume 102, Issue 2 , Pages 109-124, 1 June 2001; Frans B.M. deWaal. 'Putting the Altruism Back into Altruism: The Evolution of Empathy.' Annu. Rev. Psychol. 2008. 59:279–300.

[99] Baby kindness: Bloom P. 'Morality: Infant origins of human kindness.' New Scientist, 21 October 2010, Magazine issue 2782.

[100] Hamlin JK, Wynn K, Bloom P. Social evaluation by preverbal infants. Nature 450, 557-559 (22 November 2007)

[101] Rapidly sensing others: Willis J, Todorov A. 'First Impressions: Making Up Your Mind After a 100-Ms Exposure to a Face.' Psychological Science, July 2006 17: 592-598

[102] Oliver Sachs: 'The man who mistook his wife for a hat,' 1985, p.85.

[103] Mirror neurons: Rizzolatti G, Craighero L. 'The mirror-neuron system.' Annu. Rev. Neurosci. 2004. 27:169–92; Mukamel R, Ekstrom D, Kaplan J et al. 'Single-Neuron Responses in Humans during Execution and Observation of Actions.' Current Biology 20, 750–756, April 27, 2010; Rizzolatti G, Fogassi L, Gallese V. 'Neurophysiological mechanisms underlying the understanding and imitation of action.' Neuroscience Volume 2, September 2001, 661

[104] Smile: Mukamel R, Ekstrom AD, Kaplan J, et al. Single-Neuron Responses in Humans during Execution and Observation of Actions. Current Biology 20, 750–756, April 27, 2010

[105] Mirror neurons: Rizzolatti G, Fogassi L, Gallese V. 'Neurophysiological mechanisms underlying the understanding and imitation of action.' Neuroscience Volume 2, September 2001, 661

[106] Language: Arbib MA. 'The Mirror System, Imitation, and the Evolution of Language,' in Imitation in Animals and Artifacts, (Chrystopher Nehaniv and Kerstin Dautenhahn, Editors), The MIT Press. 2000

[107] Reading the minds of geometric shapes: Heider F, Simmel M. 'An experimental study of apparent behavior.' The American Journal of Psychology. 1944, V57(2), 243-

[108] Anti-Castro debaters:. Jones EE, Harris VA. (1967). 'The attribution of attitudes.' Journal of Experimental Social Psychology 3, 1–24; Gilbert DT, Malone PS. 'The Correspondence Bias.' Psychological Bulletin, 1995, Vol. 117, No. 1,21-38

[109] The honeybee waggle dance: Von Frisch K. 1993. 'The dance language and orientation of bees.' Harvard Univ Press;

Also Seeley TD. (2001). 'Decision making in superorganisms: How collective wisdom arises from the poorly informed masses.' In G. Gigerenzer & R. Selten (Eds.), 'Bounded rationality: The adaptive toolbox' The MIT Press. p. 249–261c

[110] Humans cooperate: Fehr and Gächter (2002) , cited Pfister HR, Böhm G. 'The multiplicity of emotions: A framework of emotional functions in decision making.' Judgment and Decision Making, Vol. 3, No. 1, January 2008, pp. 5–17

[111] Don Kay, an extraordinary guy

[112] The thing about people is that they want to believe you: This American Life. '447: The Incredible Case of the P.I. Moms Transcript.' 23 Sep 2011. Chicago Public Media & Ira Glass

[113] We empathise if they are not to blame: Weiner B. (1993). 'On sin versus sickness.' American Psychologist, 48, 967-985.

[114] If there are personal details: Newman TB. 'It's good to talk: The power of stories over statistics.' BMJ 2003;327:1424-1427

[115] If we see their face: Burnham, 2003; cited Aguiar F, Brañas-Garza P, Miller LM. 'Moral distance in dictator games.' Judgment and Decision Making, Vol. 3, No. 4, April 2008, pp. 344–354

[116] Males are bad at reading 'the mind in the eyes': Woolley AW, Chabris CF, Pentland A, et al. 'Evidence for a Collective Intelligence Factor in the Performance of Human Groups.' Science, published online September 30, 2010. Science DOI: 10.1126/science.1193147; little boys are too - Zahn-Waxler C, Robinson J.L & Emde RN. (1992). 'The development of empathy in twins.' Developmental Psychology, 28, 1038-1047.

[117] Doctors discriminate against those who are different and those they dislike: USA doctors. Green AR et al (2007). 'Implicit bias among physicians and its prediction of thrombolysis decisions for black and white patients.' Journal of General Internal Medicine; DOI 10.1007/s11606-007-0258-5; Swiss doctors - Escher M. Perneger TV, Chevrolet J-C. 'National questionnaire survey on what influences doctors' decisions about admission to intensive care.' BMJ 2004;329:425 (21 August), doi:10.1136/bmj.329.7463.425. Incidentally, studies show that female doctors like their patients more, and patients like female doctors more; liking your doctor is also associated with better health. Hence, it may be wise to have a female doctor! See Groopman J. 'How Doctor's Think.' Mariner Books. 2008.

[118] Framingham Heart Study: Fowler JH, Christakis NA. 'Dynamic spread of happiness in a large social network: longitudinal analysis over 20 years in the Framingham Heart Study.' BMJ 2008;337:a2338; Christakis NA. Fowler JH. 'The Collective Dynamics of Smoking in a Large Social Network.' N Engl J Med 2008; 358:2249-2258 May 22, 2008

[119] Group pressure: Brainstorming. Mullen B, Johnson C, Salas E. 'Productivity Loss in Brainstorming Groups: A Meta-Analytic Integration. Basic and Applied Social Psychology,' 1991, 12(1), 3-23; longest line, most attractive face - Asch, S.E. (1955). 'Opinions and social pressure.' Scientific American, 193, 35–35; Klucharev V., Hytonen K, Rijpkema M, Smidts A, Fernandez G. 'Reinforcement learning signal predicts social conformity.' Neuron. 2009. Vol. 61. No. 1. P. 140-151.

[120] Policies of our political party: Cohen L. 'Party Over Policy: The Dominating Impact of Group Influence on

Political Beliefs.' Journal of Personality and Social Psychology, Vol 85(5), Nov 2003, 808-822

[121] Electric shocks: Milgram S. "Behavioral Study of Obedience". Journal of Abnormal and Social Psychology. 67 (4): 371–8; 1983

[122] Engelmann et al. Expert Financial Advice Neurobiologically 'Offloads' Financial Decision-Making under Risk. PLoS ONE, 2009, 4 (3)

[123] Deference can mean tragedy: Krakauer J. ' Into thin air.' Anchor books, Random house, inc. New York, 1997. P. 196.

[124] Healthcare: UK Bristol Hospital. Mr Tony Giddings, National Clinical Assessment Authority. 'The Changing Operating Theatre'. In: 'Humans in Complex Engineering Systems'. Sharing good practice workshop. Published by The Royal Academy of Engineering, December 2004; also Sarah-Kate Templeton and Jane Feinmann. "Arrogant surgeons risk another Bristol babies scandal" The Sunday TimesSeptember 3, 2006

[125] Buist M, Harrison J, Abaloz E, Van Dyke S. 'Six year audit of cardiac arrests and medical emergency team calls in an Australian outer metropolitan teaching hospital' BMJ 2007; 335;1210-1212, originally published online 29 Nov 2007

[126] Stoicism: see Marcus Aurelius 'Meditations'.

[127] Speaking up and Israel good ideas: Senor D, Singer S. 'Start-Up Nation: The Story of Israel's Economic Miracle' 2009; also Glassman J.'Where Tech Keeps Booming',Wall Street Journal. November 23, 2009.

[128] Aviation: HumanFactors Digest No. 2 "Flight Crew Training: Cockpit Resource Management (CRM) and Line-Oriented Flight Training (LOFT)" UK Civil Aviation Authority. 2002; Sexton JB, Thomas EJ, Helmreich RL.

'Error, stress, and teamwork in medicine and aviation: cross sectional surveys,' BMJ 2000;320;745-749

[129] Efforts to implement flatter structures in UK healthcare: In process and mixed results - an international survey found little more than half of consultant surgeons believed they should be approachable by junior ones, Sexton JB, Thomas EJ, Helmreich RL. 'Error, stress, and teamwork in medicine and aviation: cross sectional surveys,' BMJ 2000;320;745-749; a high-rate of autocracy continues to be reported . Flin et al 2006. 'Attitudes to teamwork and safety in the operating theatre'. Surgeon, 1 June 2006 145-151; Giddings AFB, Williamson C. ' The Leadership and Management of Surgical Teams'. The Royal College of Surgeons England'. May 2007; P McCulloch, A Mishra1, A Handa1, T Dale, G Hirst, K Catchpole. 'The effects of aviation-style non-technical skills training on technical performance and outcome in the operating theatre.' Qual Saf Health Care 2009;18:109-115; On the other hand improved operation of medical emergency teams has been reported, when there was an empowering of junior staff to call the team and a flattening of the hierarchy with more senior staff obliged to attend the patient's bedside on request. Kathryn M Rowan, David A Harrison, 'Recognising and responding to acute illness in patients in hospital,' BMJ 2007;335:1165-1166

[130] Women are better: More likely to put others first, Whitehead M, Petticrew M, Graham H, et al. 'Evidence for public health policy on inequalities 2: Assembling the evidence jigsaw.' J.Epidemiol. Community Health. 2004;58:817-821; better at problem solving in groups in tasks such as brainstorming, making collective moral judgments, and negotiating over limited resources. See Woolley AW, Chabris CF, Pentland A, et al. 'Evidence for a Collective

Intelligence Factor in the Performance of Human Groups.' Science, published online September 30, 2010. Science DOI: 10.1126/science.1193147

131 Xuanzang: Tansen Sen. 'The Travel Records of Chinese Pilgrims Faxian, Xuanzang, and Yijing,' Sources for cross-cultural encounters between ancient china and ancient india. p. 24, Education about Asia, Volume 11, Number 3 Winter 2006

132 Women when CEOs: Cassells R, Duncan A (2020), 'Gender Equity Insights 2020: Delivering the Business Outcomes,' BCEC|WGEA Gender Equity Series, Issue #5, March 2020

133 Islamic commemoration, the day of Ashura

134 Israeli Minister & 'the curse of xenophobia': de Waal F, 'The Evolution of Empathy.' Greater Good Science Center, UC Berkeley Fall/Winter 2005-06

135 Quote: de Wall F. 'The empathic Ape'. NewScientist 8 October 2005

136 'A character of King Charles II'.By George Savile Halifax

137 Happiness and genetics: Weiss A, Bates TC, Luciano M. 'Happiness is a personal(ity) thing: the genetics of personality and well-being in a representative sample.' Psychol Sci. 2008 Mar;19(3):205-10; Bartels M, Boomsma DI. 'Born to be happy? The etiology of subjective well-being.' Behav Genet. 2009 Nov;39(6):605-15; David Lykken and Auke Tellegen. 'Happiness Is a Stochastic Phenomenon.' Psychological Science Vol.7, No. 3, May 1996

138 Happiness with age: Blanchflower DG, Oswald AJ. 'Antidepressants and Age in 27 European Countries: Evidence of a U-Shape in Human Well-being Through Life.' March 2012. Downloaded from www.andrewoswald.com/docs/newAntiDepressants15Marc

h2012.pdf on 18 November 2013; emotional reactivity when older - Seider BH, Shiota MN, Whalen P, Levenson RW. 'Greater sadness reactivity in late life.' Soc Cogn Affect Neurosci (2010) First published online: July 22, 2010

[139] David Hume: 'An Enquiry Concerning the Principles of Morals', 1777/1960, p. 131 "the ultimate ends of human actions can never, in any case, be accounted for by reason, but recommend themselves entirely to the sentiments and affections of mankind, without any dependence on the intellectual faculties". See http://www.davidhume.org/

[140] Zajonc 1980, cited Slovic, Finucane et al 2002: 'Rational Actors or Rational Fools? Implications of the Affect Heuristic for Behavioral Economics,' prepared for "Behavioral Economics and Neoclassical Economics: Continuity or Discontinuity?", the Second Annual Symposium on the Foundation of the Behavioral Sciences, sponsored by the American Institute for Economic Research, Great Barrington, Massachusetts, July 19-21, 2002.

[141] Damasio. Descarte's Error. Vintage 2006; P. XII, in Bechara A. 'The role of emotion in decision-making: evidence from neurological patients with orbitofrontal damage.' Brain Cogn. 2004 Jun;55(1):30-40; Dolan RJ. Emotion, Cognition, and Behavior. Science 298, 1191 (2002); Pfister HR, Böhm G. 'The multiplicity of emotions: A framework of emotional functions in decision making.' Judgment and Decision Making, Vol. 3, No. 1, January 2008, pp. 5–17

[142] Mental time traveling: Quoidbach J, Hansenne M, Mottet C. 'Personality and mental time travel: A differential approach to autonoetic consciousness.' Consciousness and Cognition 17 (2008) 1082–1092

[143] Harry Evans: 'Time, Chance and Parliament: Lessons From Forty Years'. Papers on Parliament. Lectures in the Senate Occasional Lecture Series, and other papers. June 2010. Published and printed by the Department of the Senate, Parliament House, Canberra ISSN 1031–976X.

[144] Paul Klugman: Gittins R, 'Why economists failed to predict a train wreck'. Sydney Morning Herald, Sep 12, 2009

[145] Kuhnen CM, Knutson B. 'The Influence of Affect on Beliefs, Preferences, and Financial Decisions. Journal of financial and quantitative analysis.' Vol. 46, No. 3, June 2011, pp. 605–626

[146] Economic down turns: Tolnay SE, Beck EM. 'A festival of violence: An analysis of southern lynchings,' 1882-1930, 1995

[147] The benefits of self control, the Dunedin Study: Moffitt TE, Arseneault L, Belsky D, et al. 'A gradient of childhood self-control predicts health, wealth, and public safety' PNAS February 15, 2011 108 (7) 2693-2698;

[148] Reference Dependence: Kahneman & Tversky, 1979; 'Reference dependence' thought experiment adapted from example given in Kahneman D, 'A Perspective on Judgment and Choice - Mapping Bounded Rationality' September 2003, American Psychologist, p. 697 - ; reference dependence became a primary element of 'Prospect Theory,' and its successor cumulative prospect theory. Prospect theory replaced 'expected utility theory' which assumed absolute not relative value. Developed by Kahneman and Tversky, prospect theory became the dominant theory describing decision making under conditions of uncertainty. It applies to states in general, including money, health, and relationships. Michael H. Birnbaum. 'New Paradoxes of

Risky Decision Making.' Psychological Review , 2008, Vol. 115, No. 2, 463–501

149 Loss Aversion: Baucells M, 'A Survey Study of Factors Influencing Risk-Taking Behavior in Real-World Decisions Under Uncertainty.' Decision Analysis, Vol. 3, No. 3, September 2006, pp. 163–176; Futures and options traders also show loss aversion, which is a problem as it can leads to severe counter-productive trading when a loss is detected in place of relying on benefitting over time (traders are worse at this than undergraduate students. Haigh MS, List JA. 'Do Professional Traders Exhibit Myopic Loss Aversion? An Experimental Analysis,' The Journal of Finance. Vol. LX, No. 1 , February 2005; Banks SM, Salovey P, Greener S, et al. 'The effects of message framing on mammography utilization.' Health Psychology. Vol 14(2), Mar 1995, 178-184.

150 Redelmeier: Redelmeier DA, Kahneman D. 'Patients' memories of painful medical treatments: real-time and retrospective evaluations of two minimally invasive procedures.' Pain, 66 (1996)3-8.

151 Guyse JL, Keller LR, Eppel T. 'Valuing environmental outcomes: Preferences for constant or improving sequences.' Organizational behavior and human decision processes. 2002. 87(2):253-277.

152 Diener E, Wirtz D, Oishi S. 'End effects of rated life quality: The James Dean effect.' 2001. Psychological science, 12(2):124-128

153 Stradivarius violins: Marchese J (2008). 'The Violin Maker: A Search for the Secrets of Craftsmanship, Sound, and Stradivari.' First Harper Perennial Edition 2008. pp.133–134

[154] Fritz C, Curtin J, Poitevineau J et al. Player preferences among new and old violins. PNAS Proceedings of the National Academy of Sciences of the United States of America, Published online before print January 3, 2012, doi: 10.1073/pnas.1114999109 PNAS

[155] Wine: Goldstein R, Almenberg J, et al. 'Do More Expensive Wines Taste Better? Evidence from a Large Sample of Blind Tastings.' American Association of wine economists, AAWE Working paper. No. 16, April 2008

[156] Placebo Affect: Benedetti F, Maggi G, Lopiano L, et al. 'Open versus hidden medical treatments: The patient's knowledge about a therapy affects the therapy outcome.' Prevention & Treatment. Vol 6(1), Jun 2003, ArtID 1a.; Waber RL, Shiv B, Carmon Z, Ariely D. 'Commercial features of placebo 1 and therapeutic efficacy.' JAMA 2008;299:1016-7. Also cited by Spiegel D, Willson AH. 'What is the placebo worth? The doctor-patient relationship is a crucial part of its value.' BMJ 2008;336:967-8 ; Kaptchuk TJ, Stason WB, Davis RB, et al. 'Sham device v inert pill: randomised controlled trial of two placebo treatments.' BMJ 2006 332: 391-397.

[157] 'Nocebo Affect.' Montogomery, cited by Pilcher H in 'The Science of Voodoo: When Mind Attacks Body.' NewScientist magazine, May 15, 2009.

[158] Positive beliefs ward off illness: Optimistic temperament in nuns, see Danner DD, Snowdon DA, Friesen WV, 'Positive Emotions in Early Life and Longevity: Findings from the Nun Study.' Journal of Personality and Social Psychology, 2001, Vol. 80, No. 5, 804-813.

[159] Beneficail effects of religion: Kendler KS, Karkowski LM, Prescott CA. Causal Relationship Between Stressful Life Events and the Onset of Major Depression. Am J Psychiatry 156:837-841, June 1999; Inzlicht M, McGregor I,. Hirsh JB et

al. 'Neural Markers of Religious Conviction.' Psychological Science March 2009 vol. 20 no. 3 385-392; Callaway C. 'Religious people less anxious, brain activity shows.' 17 March 2009. New Scientist.

160 Belief gives success in one's career: TavaniCM, Losh SC. 'Motivation, self-confidence, and expectations as predictors of the academic performances among our high school students.' Child Study Journal. Vol 33(3), 2003, 141-151.; Marsh H, Chanal JP, Sarrazin PG. 'Self-belief does make a difference: A reciprocal effects model of the causal ordering of physical self-concept and gymnastics performance.' Journal of Sports Sciences. Vol 24(1), Jan 2006, 101-111.; Kjormo O, Halvari H. 'Two ways related to performance in elite sport: The path of self-confidence and competitive anxiety and the path of group cohesion and group goal-clarity.' Perceptual and Motor Skills. Vol 94(3,Pt1), Jun 2002, 950-966.

161 Helen Keller: 'Optimism, An Essay.' Published November, 1903. D. B. Updike, The Merrymount Press, Boston. See: http://www.gutenberg.org/files/31622/31622-h/31622-h.htm

162 Hope is most valuable: Amnesty International Australia: News letter from Amnesty International Australia, 19 Feb 2015, from actioncentre@amnesty.org.au; Birenbaum H. 'Hope is the last to die: A coming of age under nazi terror.' M. E. Sharpe, Armonk New York, 1996 P.178

163 Nothing is either good or bad: Shakespeare, 'Hamlet'. Act 2 Scene 2.

164 Believing things we know to be untrue: Orwell G. 'In Front of Your Nose', Tribune. GB, London. March 22, 1946

165 Explaining why the future will be good: Note that no one knows the future - a history professor once described to me

the events that led to Australia's current state. I listened, smirked, and replied. 'If historians understand how one event leads to another, perhaps you could tell us who is going to win the next election?' 'Well,' he said, 'In our field of study, we historians do have the advantage of knowing what happened next!' We only know the future once it has occurred.

[166] All make adjustments to view circumstances positively: 'Students on date' Wilson TD, Wheatley TP, Kurtz JL, Dunn EW, Gilbert DT. 'When to fire: anticipatory versus postevent reconstrual of uncontrollable events.' Pers Soc Psychol Bull. 2004 Mar;30(3):340-51; 'Expanded US Base' Silvia Galdi, Luciano Arcuri, Bertram Gawronski. 'Choices of Undecided Decision-Makers Automatic Mental Associations Predict Future.' Science. 1100 (2008); 321

[167] Talking therapies: Steven D. Hollon, Michael O. Stewart, and Daniel Strunk. 'Enduring Effects for Cognitive Behavior Therapy in the Treatment of Depression and Anxiety.' Annu. Rev. Psychol. 2006. 57:285–315

[168] For a motivational book, try Wayne Dyer's 'Your erroneous zones'.

[169] A woman in Berlin: Anonymous. 'A Woman In Berlin'. Virago Modern Classics, Published 25th October 2011

[170] Majdanek death camp: Birenbaum H. 'Hope is the last to die: A coming of age under nazi terror.' M. E. Sharpe, Armonk New York, 1996

[171] Ocean sailer: Mulville F. 'Single handed cruising and sailing'. Nautical, Macmillan London Ltd. 1981.

[172] Suppression by the severely ill: Adang EMM, Kootstra G, van Hoeff JP et al. 'Do retrospective and prospective quality of life assessments differ for pancreas-kidney transplant recipients'. Transplant Intenational 11:11-5. (1998); Everts

B, Karlson B, Wahrborg P et al. (1999). ' Pain recollection after chest pain of cardiac origin.' Cardiology, 92(2):115-120 ; Breme K, Altmeppen J, Taeger K. (2000). 'How reliable is our memory for acute postoperative pain.' Anaesthetist, 49(1):18-24

173 Hot/cold empathy gap: Unpublished paper by Loewenstein G, Schkade D. 'Wouldn't It Be Nice? Predicting Future Feelings' 1997

174 Oliver Sacks on narratives: Sacks O. 'The man who mistook his wife for a hat.' 1985

175 Von Moltke on changing plans: In "On Strategy" (1871), Hughes DJ, Bell H. 'Moltke on the Art of War: Selected Writings' (1993)

176 Invasion and occupation of Australia: Robinson, G.A., 1839-49, Journals, Port Phillip Protectorate, Mitchell Library, State Library of New South Wales, cited by Clark ID, 'Scars in the Landscape: A register of Massacre Sites in Western Victoria', 1803 - 1859, Pages 145 – 152, Aboriginal Studies Press, 1995.

177 Einstein: 'The real problem is in the hearts of men'. Title of interview with Michael Amrinc published in the Sunday Magazine section of the New York Times on 23 June 1946, as reported in 'Einstein on Politics: His Private Thoughts and Public Stands on Nationalism, Zionism, War, Peace, and the Bomb', Edited David E. Rowe & Robert Schulmann, Princeton University Press, 2007 "It is easier to denature plutonium than to denature the evil heart of man".

178 Vollset SE, Goren E, Yuan CW et al. 'Fertility, mortality, migration, and population scenarios for 195 countries and territories from 2017 to 2100: a forecasting analysis for the Global Burden of Disease Study.' The Lancet. Open Access. Published July 14, 2020

[179] UN report on Intergovernmental Science-Policy Platform on Biodiversity and Ecosystem Services (IPBES), 7th session of the IPBES Plenary meeting 1 (29 April – 4 May), Paris 2019

[180] UN Climate Action Summit, UN Secretary-General António Guterres closing words. 23 September 2019

[181] See Global Alliance for the Rights of Nature (GARN) website, https://therightsofnature.org/ecuador-rights/ , accessed on 6 June 2020 along with Ecuador Constitution of 2008 at https://pdba.georgetown.edu/Constitutions/Ecuador/english08.html

[182] River having the rights of a human. https://www.npr.org/sections/thetwo-way/2017/03/16/520414763/a-new-zealand-river-now-has-the-legal-rights-of-a-human

[183] Cancer patients report satisfied but clinically depressed: VanderZee K, Buunk B, De Ruiter J. 1996. 'Social comparison and the subjective well-being of cancer patients.' Basic and Applies Social Psychology. 18(4): 453-468

[184] Patient views differ from family members: Epstein AM, Hall JA, Tognetti J et al. 1989. 'Using proxies to evaluate quality of life.' Medical Care 27(3):S91-S98

[185] Lewis Carroll: Lewis Carroll (1893) 'Curiosa Mathematica'; Richard M. Wenzlaff and Daniel M. Wegner. 'Thought Suppression.' Annu. Rev. Psychology. 2000. 51:59–91

[186] Women with breast cancer: Gilbar O, Hevroni A. 'Counterfactuals, coping strategies and psychological distress among breast cancer patients.' Published in: Anxiety, Stress & Coping, Volume 20, Issue 4 December 2007 , pages 383 –

[187] Quote 'simply by putting' by Haidt: See Jonathan Haidt: The Emotional Dog and Its Rational Tail: A Social Intuitionist Approach to Moral Judgment. Psychological Review, 2001. Vol. 108. No. 4, 814-834. Also: de Waal F. 'The Antiquity of Empathy.' Science 18 May 2012: Vol. 336 no. 6083 pp. 874-876; de Waal FBM, 'The Evolution of Empathy.' Greater Good Science Center, UC Berkeley Fall/Winter 2005-06

[188] My two year old daughter was very fond of slaters, small multi-legged, land-living crustaceans found all over Australia. She called them 'beachy boys' and carried them in her pockets, and was upset when they 'broke'

[189] Animals caring for their own: Bekoff M. "Do animals have emotions?" New Scientist, 23 May 2007; Hecht EE, Patterson R, Barbey AK. "What can other animals tell us about human social cognition? An evolutionary perspective on reflective and reflexive processing." Front Hum Neurosci. 2012;6:224 Jul 27; de Waal FBM. "The Antiquity of Empathy." Science 18 May 2012: Vol. 336 no. 6083 pp. 874-876

[190] Mice empathy: Langford DJ, Crager SE, Shehzad Z, Smith SB, Sotocinal SG, Levenstadt JS, Chanda ML, Levitin DJ, and Mogil JS. 2006. 'Social Modulation of Pain as Evidence for Empathy in Mice. Science.' 312(5782):1967-70.

[191] Rats share their food: Bartal IBA, Decety J, Mason P. 'Empathy and Pro-Social Behavior in Rats.' Science, Vol. 334 Issue 6061, Dec. 9, 2011. Vol. 334 no. 6061 pp. 1427-1430

[192] Rhesus monkeys won't shock others: Masserman JH. Wechkin S, and Terris W. 1964. '"Altruistic" behavior in rhesus monkeys.' American Journal of Psychiatry 121: 584-585.

[193] Pimate mind-reading: Wellman HM, Brandone AC. 'Early intention understandings that are common to primates predict children's later theory of mind.' Current Opinion in

Neurobiology 2009, 19:57–62; Platt ML, Spelke ES. What can developmental and comparative cognitive neuroscience tell us about the adult human brain? Current Opinion in Neurobiology 2009, 19:1–5

[194] Scrub Jays hide if they steal: Emery NJ, Clayton NS. 'Effects of experience and social context on prospective caching strategies by scrub jays.' Nature 414, 443-446, 22 November 2001; Stulp G, Emery N J, Verhulst S. & Clayton N S. (2009). 'Western scrub-jays conceal auditory information when competitors can hear but cannot see.' Proceedings of the Royal Society of London Series B Biological Letters 5, 583-585 ; Emery NJ, Clayton NS, Frith CD. 'Social intelligence: from brain to culture.' Phil. Trans. R. Soc. B 2007 362, 485-488

[195] Kohler's apes: Corballis MC. 'From Hand to Mouth: The Origins of Language,' Princeton University Press 2002; Kohler, 1925, p. 38, cited Robert Epstein 'Generativity Theory and Creativity'. In 'Theories of creativity', Edited Mark A. Runco and Robert S. Albert, Sage Publications, 1990

[196] Crows with tools: Hunt GR, Corballis MC, Gray RD. 'Laterality in tool manufacture by crows.' Nature, Dec 13, 2001, p707

[197] Octopus: Mather JA. 'Cephalopod consciousness: Behavioural evidence.' Consciousness and Cognition, Volume 17, Issue 1, March 2008, Pages 37-48

[198] Number: Kinzler KD, Spelke ES. 'Core systems in human cognition.' In: C. von Hofsten & K. Rosander (Eds.) Progress in Brain Research, Vol. 164 2007

[199] Sleep: Lesku JA, Roth TC, Rattenborg NC, et al. 'Phylogenetics and the correlates of mammalian sleep: A reappraisal.' Sleep Medicine Reviews, Volume 12, Issue 3 , Pages 229-244, June 2008

[200] Dogs: Correa JE. 'The Dog's Sense of Smell.' Alabama Cooperative Extension System, UNP-0066, Alabama A&M and Auburn Universities, 2011

[201] Kleinlogel S, White AG (2008) 'The Secret World of Shrimps: Polarisation Vision at Its Best.' PLoS ONE 3(5): e2190

[202] Ashoka: See Sighal DP. 'India and World Civilisation.' Sidgwick & Jackson, London 1972. Also https://en.wikipedia.org/wiki/Ashoka

[203] Weighing a heart: Carelli F. 'The book of death: weighing your heart.' London J Prim Care (Abingdon). 2011 Jul; 4(1): 86–87

[204] Quote: 'Know thyself.' Pausanias (10.24.1). 'Description of Greece.' Translated by Jones WHS and Omerod HA. Loeb Classical Library Volumes. Cambridge, MA, Harvard University Press; London, William Heinemann Ltd. 1918. See http://www.theoi.com/Text/Pausanias10B.html#2

[205] Flawed creatures: McEwen I. 'A Boot Room in The Frozen North'. McEwan 2005.html. "But we will not rescue the earth from our own depredations until we understand ourselves a little more, even if we accept that we can never really change our natures. All boot rooms need good systems so that flawed creatures can use them well. Good science will serve us well, but only good rules will save the boot room. Leave nothing to idealism or outrage, or even good art. (We know in our hearts that the very best art is entirely and splendidly useless)". Ian McEwan, Copyright 2005. Written following the Cape Farewell 2005 art/science expedition which joined the Noorderlicht locked in ice at Tempelfjorden, Svalbard just north of the 79th parallel.

[206] Can our intelligence save us?: David Attenborough. 'How Many People Can Live on Planet Earth?' BBC Horizon, 2009.

'It's clear that we'll have to change the way that we live and use our resources. ... Can our intelligence save us? I hope so.

207 Wilson C. 'The mind parasites.' 1967

208 quoting from his mentor, the New South Wales Premier Jack Lang

209 Things hidden: Wittgenstein L. 'Philosophical Investigations' 1953

210 False axioms: 'Autobiographical notes,' written by Einstein in 1946, and published in 1949; see 'Einstein Chases a Light Beam', Galina Weinstein - arXiv preprint arXiv:1204.1833, 2012 - arxiv.org

211 Politicians require this most of all, it is they who determine legislation and government policy, and their mistakes are the most damaging.

212 World population: There are positive signs - the human population growth rate is declining due to decreasing world fertility rates. See 'World Population Prospects 2019: Highlights.' June 2019. United Nations, Department of Economic and Social Affairs, Population Division. https://population.un.org/wpp

213 Animal numbers have halved in forty years, while the number of people has doubled: see https://www.theguardian.com/environment/2014/sep/29/earth-lost-50-wildlife-in-40-years-wwf

214 Leave half of the world to nature: Wilson EO. 'Half-Earth: Our Planet's Fight for Life.' W W Norton & Company. 2017

215 A Global Deal For Nature, Guiding principles, milestones, and targets.' Dinerstein E. Vynne C, Sala E, et al. Science Advances. 19 Apr 2019: Vol. 5, no. 4,

216 Valuing man and nature equally: Helen George. 'Meet Burnham Beeches: an Important Ecosystem Shaped by Traditional Farming.' July 27, 2019

https://www.earthlawcenter.org/blog-entries/2019/7/meet-burnham-beeches-an-important-ecosystem-shaped-by-traditional-farming

[217] Gus Speth: See Crockett D. (Aug 22, 2014). "Connection Will Be the Next Big Human Trend". Huffington Post.

[218] Friedrich Nietzsche "Beyond Good and Evil"

Made in the USA
Monee, IL
20 September 2020